Day Hike!
MOUNT RAINIER

2nd Edition

Ron C. Judd
with Seabury Blair, Jr.

SASQUATCH BOOKS
SEATTLE

Printed in the United States of America
Published by Sasquatch Books
Distributed by PGW/Perseus
15 14 13 12 11 10 09   9 8 7 6 5 4 3 2 1

Cover design: Rosebud Eustace
Cover photograph: Don Paulson, www.donpaulson.com
Interior design: Jenny Wilkson
Interior composition: Emily Ford
Interior photographs: Ron C. Judd and Seabury Blair, Jr.
Maps: Marlene Blair

Library of Congress Cataloging-in-Publication Data

Judd, Ron C.
    Day hike! Mount Rainier : the best trails you can hike in a day / Ron C. Judd with Seabury Blair, Jr. -- 2nd ed.
        p. cm.
    Includes index.
    ISBN-13: 978-1-57061-598-6
    ISBN-10: 1-57061-598-5
    1. Hiking--Washington (State)--Mount Rainier National Park--Guidebooks. 2. Trails--Washington (State)--Mount Rainier National Park--Guidebooks. 3. Mount Rainier National Park (Wash.)--Guidebooks. I. Blair, Seabury. II. Title.
    GV199.42.W22M6842 2009
    796.5109797'782--dc21
                                                2009009490

Important Note: Please use common sense. No guidebook can act as a substitute for experience, careful planning, the right equipment, and appropriate training. There is inherent danger in all the activities described in this book, and readers must assume full responsibility for their own actions and safety. Changing or unfavorable conditions in weather, roads, trails, snow, waterways, and so forth cannot be anticipated by the author or publisher, but should be considered by any outdoor participants. The author and publisher will not be responsible for the safety of users of this guide.

Sasquatch Books
119 South Main Street, Suite 400
Seattle, WA 98104
(206) 467-4300
www.sasquatchbooks.com
custserv@sasquatchbooks.com

CONTENTS

CONTENTS

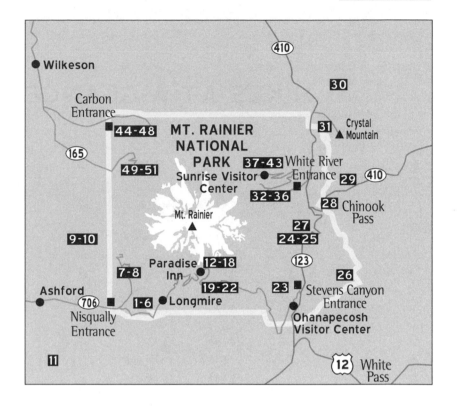

HIKES AT A GLANCE

Easy

NO.	HIKE NAME	RATING	BEST SEASON	KIDS	DOGS
1	Kautz Creek	🚶🚶🚶	June–Nov	✔	
2	Twin Firs Loop	🚶🚶🚶	May–Nov	✔	
3	Trail of the Shadows	🚶🚶🚶	June–Nov	✔	
5	Carter/Madcap Falls	🚶🚶🚶	July–Oct	✔	
7	Round Pass	🚶🚶🚶🚶	Aug–Sept	✔	✔
9	Goat Lake	🚶🚶🚶🚶	Aug–Sept	✔	✔
12	Nisqually Vista	🚶🚶🚶🚶🚶	mid-July–mid-Aug	✔	
16	Paradise to Narada Falls	🚶🚶🚶	mid-July–mid-Aug	✔	
24	Grove of the Patriarchs	🚶🚶🚶🚶🚶	June–Oct	✔	
25	Silver Falls Loop	🚶🚶🚶🚶	May–Oct	✔	
28	Naches Peak Loop	🚶🚶🚶🚶🚶	late July–mid-Aug	✔	✔
34	Emmons Moraine	🚶🚶🚶🚶	July–Sept	✔	
36	Silver Forest/Emmons Vista	🚶🚶🚶	mid-July–mid-Aug	✔	
37	Sunrise Rim Loop	🚶🚶🚶🚶	mid-July–mid-Sept	✔	
38	Sourdough Ridge/Dege Peak	🚶🚶🚶	mid-July–mid-Aug	✔	

Moderate

NO.	HIKE NAME	RATING	BEST SEASON	KIDS	DOGS
4	Rampart Ridge Loop	🚶🚶	Sept–Oct	✔	
8	Lake George	🚶🚶🚶	Sept–Oct	✔	✔
10	Glacier View	🚶🚶🚶🚶	mid-July–mid-Aug	✔	✔
17	Upper Paradise Valley	🚶🚶🚶🚶	July–Aug	✔	
18	Paradise Glacier	🚶🚶🚶🚶	mid-July–Sept	✔	
19	High Lakes Loop	🚶🚶🚶🚶	mid-July–mid-Aug	✔	
21	Bench and Snow Lakes	🚶🚶🚶	mid-July–Sept	✔	
27	Eastside Trail	🚶🚶🚶	Aug–Sept	✔	
32	Owyhigh Lakes	🚶🚶🚶🚶	July–Sept	✔	
33	Summerland	🚶🚶🚶🚶🚶	late July–Sept	✔	
34	Glacier Basin	🚶🚶🚶🚶	July–Sept		

39	Huckleberry Creek/Forest Lake	🚶🚶	mid-July–Sept	✔
40	Frozen Lake/Mount Fremont Lookout	🚶🚶🚶🚶	mid-July–mid-Sept	✔
42	Berkeley Park	🚶🚶🚶	Aug	✔
43	Skyscraper Pass	🚶🚶🚶	Aug–Sept	✔
44	Green Lake	🚶🚶🚶	Aug–Sept	✔
46	Carbon Glacier Viewpoint	🚶🚶🚶🚶	Aug–Sept	✔
51	Spray Park	🚶🚶🚶🚶🚶	late July–Aug	✔

Moderately Difficult

NO.	HIKE NAME	RATING	BEST SEASON	KIDS	DOGS
6	Comet Falls	🚶🚶🚶🚶	mid-July–mid-Aug	✔	
11	High Rock Lookout	🚶🚶🚶	July–Aug	✔	✔
13	Alta Vista	🚶🚶🚶🚶	July–Aug	✔	
20	Pinnacle Saddle	🚶🚶🚶🚶	Aug–Sept	✔	
22	Stevens Creek	🚶🚶	June–Oct		
29	Sheep Lake	🚶🚶🚶	Aug	✔	✔
30	Noble Knob	🚶🚶🚶🚶	Aug	✔	✔
31	Crystal Lakes	🚶🚶🚶🚶	Aug–Sept	✔	
35	Palisades Lakes	🚶🚶🚶	mid-July–mid-Aug		
41	Burroughs Mountain	🚶🚶🚶🚶🚶	mid-Aug–mid-Sept		
49	Mowich River Camp	🚶🚶🚶🚶	Aug–Sept	✔	

Difficult

NO.	HIKE NAME	RATING	BEST SEASON	KIDS	DOGS
1	Indian Henry's Hunting Ground	🚶🚶🚶	July–Sept		
6	Van Trump Park	🚶🚶🚶🚶	mid-July–mid-Aug		
14	Panorama Point/Skyline Loop	🚶🚶🚶🚶🚶	Aug		
23	Cowlitz Divide	🚶🚶🚶🚶	July–Sept		
26	Three Lakes	🚶🚶🚶🚶	Sept		
45	Really Big Tree/Ipsut Pass	🚶	Aug	✔	
47	Cataract Camp/Seattle Park	🚶🚶	July–Sept		
48	Yellowstone Cliffs	🚶	Sept		
50	Tolmie Peak	🚶🚶🚶	Aug		

Extreme

NO.	HIKE NAME	RATING	BEST SEASON	KIDS	DOGS
15	Camp Muir	🚶🚶🚶🚶	July–Aug		

ACKNOWLEDGMENTS

The author is indebted to longtime friend, mentor, and misguided-trek partner Seabury Blair, Jr., who walked, measured, and catalogued many of the trails in this guide when the author's knee got cranky. Thanks also to everyone who loves Mount Rainier enough to keep it special—which it truly is.

—Ron C. Judd

ABOUT THE AUTHOR

Washington-state native Ron C. Judd, a veteran columnist at *The Seattle Times*, has spent most of his life exploring the trails, campgrounds, streams, and beaches of the Pacific Northwest. The author of a half dozen best-selling guidebooks, two humor books, and a fan's guide to the Winter Olympics, he lives in Bellingham, Washington. Follow his work and check for guidebook updates at www.ronjudd.com.

MOUNT RAINIER

Mount Rainier: Yeah, you've seen it.

But have you really *seen* it?

Maybe that's not the right word. You can't really say you've experienced one of North America's most stupendous peaks until you get to know the place intimately. And to know Rainier is to leave its congested parking lots and enter its wild spots, shake hands with its evergreens, breathe its crisp air, smell its wildflowers, and soak your aching feet in its cool streams.

All things, fortunately, that can easily be done on just about any two steps down one of Mount Rainier National Park's 240 magical miles of maintained trails.

We emphasize here the word "easily." One of the great misperceptions of the mountain local natives call Tahoma is that you have to be in Everest shape to partake of its 228,000 acres of pristine wilderness. This is understandable: Just *look* at the thing. The mountain is huge, forbidding, and rough-hewn. Since Rainier truly is an exposed, vertical being, much of its land is very rugged, and the terrain from its shoulders on up requires the kind of backcountry know-how you can't get by walking around Seattle's Green Lake a half-dozen times a year.

But all around this mountain's ample waistline, magic awaits. Alpine meadows too beautiful to be real. Sprawling snowfields. Stunning views. Old-growth trees, bigger than your house. Liquid-crystal rivers. Box canyons. Two dozen of the most massive glaciers on the continent. Ample wildlife.

You can see some of it without ever getting 50 feet from your car. But you can't really see it until you're in it, and the best—and only—way to get there at Mount Rainier is by foot, down a path.

That's a simple lesson we learned anew by researching this guide, which aims simply to bring to life fifty-one of the greatest walking paths in the Northwest, if not the nation, for Rainier visitors who get to the mountain once a week or once in a lifetime.

They range from the awesome—and occasionally dangerous—alpine trek to Camp Muir above Paradise to a placid, universally overlooked path winding through old-growth forest west of Longmire. Most of the trails fall somewhere in between, and all of them remind us of a delightful fact often overshadowed by the mountain's sheer size: You can get out in Mount Rainier National Park—really out, in the memory-of-a-lifetime kind of way—without committing a week of your life or ten years' wear and tear on your knees.

Almost all the hikes listed in this guide can be undertaken by the average it's-a-sunny-Sunday-morning-let's-do-something-grand hiker. Granted, some are steep, and hiking above 5,000 feet will leave the unconditioned flatlander huffing and puffing (take your time; you'll adjust). Proper preparation and attention to weather, snow levels, and other factors are important. But the fact remains that Mount Rainier National Park presents a rare opportunity for both visitors and residents. Perhaps nowhere in the world is such a unique alpine environment within such close reach of a major metropolitan area.

This explains the crowds that plague the park on summer weekends—and threaten to make today's unfettered auto access to park attractions and trailheads a thing of the past. More than two million people visit the park each year, with the vast majority landing there on summer weekends.

Being park consumers in the same way you are, we've kept that in mind in preparing this guide, attempting to warn you away from the worst overcrowding—and suggesting alternatives to popular trails when there's simply no way you can get to the park except on that same sunny August weekend with everyone else.

One of the more profound findings in our summer-long trek through the park, however, was how easily solitude or near-solitude could be attained by walking more than a couple miles from some of Rainier's most overcrowded tourist haunts. Pick a trail from the guide, follow it as far as you will, and find out for yourself. You just might discover something about a place you thought you knew—and about yourself.

WHAT'S NEW IN THE
SECOND EDITION

As usual, the largest changes in the hiking landscape at Mount Rainier between the publication of the first and second editions of this guide were brought on by nature, particularly flooding. Massive floods in the early winter of 2006 caused hundreds of millions of dollars of damage to roads, trails, and other facilities in Mount Rainier National Park. Many major roads were washed out and had to be rebuilt; footlogs and bridges were washed away from trails. And an entire campground, Sunshine Point, was physically washed away by the raging Nisqually River.

Fortunately, thanks to many hours of hard work by park staff and volunteers, most trails have been restored. Aside from one backcountry section of the Wonderland Trail (not covered in this guide), existing trails have been reopened, most on their previous routes. One notable exception is the Emmons Moraine/Glacier Basin trail (see page 132), which was washed out by the White River. Some of that hike was still accessible when this book went to press; a workaround route for the lower portion of the trail has been established, and permanent repairs are expected by 2010.

Other important changes for this edition include road access, or the possible lack thereof, to trails in the Carbon River drainage (see page xvii for more information regarding these trails). And the park opened a large new visitor center at Paradise in fall 2008 with its real tourist debut in spring 2009. At this writing, the old visitor center is scheduled for demolition. And entrance fees, both to the park and to all national parks, for those who buy an annual pass, have increased.

Changes have been made to the text and maps in the book to reflect all of these realities. We have also updated or changed contact information for many of the trails, to put you in touch more easily with park officials who work near the trailheads.

USING THIS GUIDE

The beginning of each trail description is intended to give you quick information that can help you decide whether the specific day hike is one that interests you. Here's what you'll find:

Trail Number & Name

Trails are numbered in this guide following a geographical order; see the Overview Map on page v for general location. Trail names usually reflect those names used by the national park, national forest service, and other land managers. In some cases, portions of very long trails or multiple sections of separate trails may have been combined into a single hike and assigned a new name by the author.

Overall Rating

Assigning an overall rating to a hike is a difficult task, given the fact that one hiker's preferred trail is another's dung-heap. Yet every hike in this guide is worth taking (we're still working on the dung-heap trail guide). Here, the difference between a five-star hike and one with four stars might only be the number and variety of wildflowers along the trail, or the height of the tripping tree-roots arrayed on the path before you. The trails in this book are the best you'll find at Mount Rainier. Some might not be as good as others, but they are all better than the ones we've excluded.

Another problem is attempting to be objective in rating the trails. Some of us are pushovers for trails above timberline, where the wildflowers wave in gentle summer breezes, where mountains claw clouds, where cooling snowfields linger through summer. Hikes with these features may be rated higher than you might rate them. If you're a hiker who loves walking along rattling rivers, padding on rain forest trails softened by mosses while trying to find the sky through a canopy of 300-foot-tall evergreens, you might add one star to every lowland hike listed here, and subtract one star from every alpland hike.

Finally, many factors must be considered in assigning an overall rating. Besides all that aesthetic stuff like scenery and wildlife and Really Big Trees, there are objective criteria like trail condition, length and steepness; and obstacles like creek crossings or deadfall. On the other hand, you can forget all that junk and just take our word for it:

🥾 This hike is worth taking, even with your in-laws.

🥾🥾 Expect to discover socially and culturally redeeming values on this hike. Or, at least, very fine scenery.

🥾🥾🥾 You would be willing to get up before sunrise to take this hike, even if you watched all of Letterman the night before.

🥾🥾🥾🥾 Here is the Häagen-Dazs of hikes; if you don't like ice cream, a hike with this rating will give more pleasure than any favorite comfort food.

🥾🥾🥾🥾🥾 The aesthetic and physical rewards are so great that hikes given this rating are forbidden by most conservative religions.

Distance

The distance listed is round-trip, exclusive of any side trips to other features mentioned along the way. If these excursions off the main trail are longer than about 0.2 mile, that distance will be mentioned in the description of the hike.

Hiking Time

This is an estimate of the time it takes the average hiker to walk the trail, round-trip. Since none of us are average hikers, you may feel free to ignore this entry. For the most part, however, the pace on the trail is calculated at about 2 miles per hour. Times are estimated conservatively; even so, this rate might slow on trails with significant elevation gain. (Some hikers will wonder what sort of trail slug came up with such ridiculously long hiking times—and we're okay with that.)

Elevation Gain

This is a calculation of the total number of feet you'll have to climb on the trail. Don't assume that all of the elevation will be gained on the way to your destination. Some of these trails actually lose elevation on the way and gain it on the return, or alternately gain and lose elevation along the way. The certainty is that on a round-trip hike, you always gain the same amount of elevation that you lose.

High Point

This is the highest point above sea level you'll reach on any given hike. In a few cases, this might be the trailhead.

Difficulty Level

Here's another tough one. Experienced hikers might find a hike rated "Moderately difficult" to be only "Moderate," while beginning trekkers might rate the same hike "Difficult." As with the hiking times, noted above, the difficulty of individual hikes was rated conservatively.

The terms used here are:

EASY: Few, if any, hills; generally between 1 and 4 miles, round-trip; suitable for families with small children.

MODERATE: Longer, gently graded hills; generally 4 to 6 miles long, round-trip.

MODERATELY DIFFICULT: Steeper grades; elevation changes greater than about 1,000 feet; between 6 and 9 miles long, round-trip.

DIFFICULT: Sustained, steep climbs of at least 1 mile; elevation gain and loss greater than 1,500 feet; usually more than 9 miles long, round-trip. Your deodorant may fail you on these.

EXTREME: Sustained steep climbs; distances greater than 10 miles, round-trip, or shorter hikes with special conditions requiring extreme care, such as loose rock or snow crossings. These trails will provide a rigorous test of your hiking skills and muscles.

Best Season

Here you'll find the season a trail typically is snow-free, followed by our recommendation for the best time of year to take any given hike. Trails that are open throughout the year or that make good three-season hikes will be noted here.

Permits/Contact

This entry will tell you whether you need any permits to hike the trail, and whom to contact for more information. Day-hiking in

Mount Rainier National Park is still free. Sort of. Most of the trails in this guide are found inside the Nisqually, Stevens Canyon, White River, and Carbon River entrances, where a day-use fee (presently $15 per carload) is collected. Frequent park visitors usually fork over $30 for an annual pass or $80 for a pass granting admission to all U.S. national parks for one year.

The park requires permits for overnight backpackers—and charges fees for advance backcountry campsite reservations. But at this writing, no permits or fees are required for day hikers. These regulations are prone to revision, though: Call before you go. Some trails in this guide fall outside national park boundaries and require the purchase of a Northwest Forest Pass or other permit; they are so noted.

Maps

The two most popular types of maps, United States Geological Survey (USGS) "quads" and Green Trails, are listed for each hike. Maps are available at outdoor retailers, park visitor centers, and from other sources. Many hikers now use Internet map servers (such as http://mapserver.maptech.com) to download USGS maps, or print their own, customized maps from CD-ROM software.

Each hike in this book includes a trail map of the route, featuring parking and trailhead, alternate routes, direction, elevation profile, and more. Our maps are based most often on USGS; use the following legend:

℗	Parking Area
————	Road
-------	Trail Route
....	Alternate Route
➤	Direction of Travel
↱	Turn Around Point
=	Bridge
5880'	Elevation

Contour Interval 40 Feet/Scale Varies

Trail Notes

Look here for a quick guide to trail regulations and features: Leashed dogs okay; off-leash dogs okay; no dogs; bikes allowed; kid-friendly; good views. Rainier hikers should note up front that pets and mountain bikes are not allowed on any trails within Mount Rainier National Park, but are allowed on a few of this guide's hikes outside park boundaries.

After the at-a-glance overview of each hike, you'll find detailed descriptions of the following:

The Hike

This section is an attempt to convey the feel of the trail in a sentence or two, including the type of trail and whether there's a one-way hiking option.

Getting There

You'll either find out how to get to the trailhead or, God forbid, become hopelessly lost. The elevation at the trailhead is also included here. Most of the trailhead directions will get you to the trailhead from the nearest national park entrance station. Here are some guidelines for getting to those entrances:

In the summer, Mount Rainier is approached by two main access routes: Highways 7 and 706 from the Puyallup/South Tacoma area (to the Nisqually Entrance, Longmire, and Paradise); and Highway 410 from Enumclaw (take Highway 18 to Enumclaw from Interstate 5) beyond Crystal Mountain Boulevard, to the White River Entrance, and Sunrise. Note that the upper portions of the latter route to Sunrise usually are not open until approximately July Fourth. Allow about 2$^{1}/_{2}$ hours from the Seattle area via either route when snow isn't a concern. Snowshoers or cross-country skiers sharp enough to turn some of this guide's hikes into winter routes should note that, in the winter, Highway 410 (Chinook Pass Highway) closes near the National Park border, at the Crystal Mountain Boulevard turnoff. That leaves Highway 706 as the only winter park entrance—the Park Service keeps the highway open to Longmire all winter, and endeavors to plow the path to Paradise every day. Chains often are required above Longmire in winter.

The park has three other summer entrances, whose opening dates vary depending on snowpack. The Stevens Canyon Entrance is on Highway 123 (Cayuse Pass Highway) on the southeast side of the park. This entrance can be reached via US 12 from the south or

Highways 410 and 123 from the east, via Enumclaw or Yakima. (Highways 410 and 123 are closed in the winter.) On the northwest side of the park, both Mowich Lake Road and Carbon River Road are unpaved entrances to the scenic (and less heavily visited) north side. Both are accessed via Highway 165, which runs south into the park from Buckley and Wilkeson. These roads are open summer only, and often are in rough condition. And their future as auto-accessible roads is in doubt.

The Carbon River Road, in particular, has been beset by natural calamities. Built below the river grade in places, the old road has washed out repeatedly. The last washout, during the deluge of park flooding that struck in November 2006, might have been the fatal blow to the road. As this book goes to press, the National Park System is mulling, once again, about the road's future as an auto entry. Several options are on the table, but none of them would reopen the road all the way to its end, 5 miles beyond the park entrance station at the former Ipsut Creek Campground, which itself was partially destroyed by the 2006 floods.

It's likely that the road will either remain closed at the current gate or partially reopen perhaps as far up the road as the Chenius Falls trailhead. If the current gate remains closed, a hiking/biking trail following the old road would run from the gate to the trailhead at Ipsut Creek Camp, where many popular day hikes—such as the trek to the snout of the Carbon Glacier—begin. (Remember, bikes are allowed only on Carbon River Road or the path replacing it, never the trails themselves.)

The road's current closure at the park entrance adds mileage that, frankly, pushes our definition of "day hikes." Hikers should be aware that once-short hikes from Ipsut Creek now will require a hike/bike trek of up to 10 miles round-trip, just getting to and from the trailhead. (A 7-mile hike from Ipsut Creek thus becomes a 17-mile hike/bike.) But because they are among some of the most spectacular hikes in the park, and because the road's fate is uncertain, we've continued to list all the Carbon River drainage trails in this guide. In this second edition, the round-trip mileages for each trail in that region have been updated to include the new road hike/bike distances to the trailheads. Always, though, check with the park for current road information before you go. Many hikers have chosen to look at the bright side about the Carbon Road: It now offers a rare opportunity to ride a mountain bike inside park boundaries, and then to hike stunning trails with much less company than in previous years. And remember: If you're on a bike, the 5 miles back out to the car are mostly downhill.

Likewise, the park's oft-washed-out West Side Road, which follows the turbulent Tahoma Creek drainage on the southwest side of the mountain, has been permanently closed by the Park Service at a large washout 3.3 miles above its beginning off Highway 706, just inside the Nisqually Entrance. An entire series of spectacular day hikes emanating from the West Side Road have thus become long walks—too long, in most cases, for the average day hiker, even if you employ a mountain bike to get from the washout to the trailhead (where the bike must be left). Much of the road has been repaired—Park Service vehicles seem to have no problems traveling it. But park managers say frequent outbursts from the South Tahoma Glacier make it too dangerous for private auto travel. A compromise may be pending: The park has proposed running a hiker's shuttle bus from the washout to popular trailheads along the route. Alas, at this guide's publication, no money to put those wheels in motion was forthcoming from the federal government. As a result, we've left some of the otherwise-grand day hikes emanating from the upper reaches of West Side Road out of this guide, because they exceed the mileage and time guidelines we've established for a day-hiking treatise. But we've included those West Side Road hikes still within a day-hiker's reach, and we've even suggested making a fun day hike out of the lower portions of the road itself (Round Pass).

Stay tuned for further developments on the West Side Road and other park access issues: The park's long-term plans also call for shuttle service to Sunrise, Paradise, the upper Mowich Lake Road, and other popular destinations—and possible auto restrictions in the same places. For updates on road conditions, call (360) 569-2211, the park's recorded information line.

The Trail

Here's where you'll get the blow-by-blow, mile-by-mile description of the trail. It's information your feet will find useful, and we apologize if, every now and then, we take time to recognize a Really Big Tree or an awesome view, since you'll probably recognize these features without much coaching.

Going Farther

In this section, you can learn about good options to take a longer hike along the same trail. Interesting side trips can be found here, too. And if there's a nearby campground that could get you on the trail sooner, or a great place to stay while exploring area trails, it also will be mentioned. Not every hike includes this section.

BE CAREFUL

It is all too easy on a warm, sunny day on the trail to forget all of the stuff you ought to be carrying in your pack. Day hikers, especially, are likely to leave that extra layer or Gore-Tex parka in the trunk. Some folks even forget that most essential item—a hiking partner. Never hike alone.

Virtually every time, day hikers who forget one or two of the basic rules for safe wilderness travel return to the trailhead smiling and healthy. No trail cop is going to cite you for negligent hiking if you have only nine of the so-called "Ten Essentials," or if you hit the trail without registering or telling someone where you're going.

Perhaps the only weighty argument anyone can make to convince another day hiker to follow the rules for safe travel in the outdoors is this: Remember the annual, avoidable tragedies that occur because hikers ignore those rules, and become news headlines instead.

The Ten Essentials

First—no matter the distance or difficulty of the hike—please carry in your pack the Ten Essentials, developed years ago by the Seattle-based mountaineering group The Mountaineers. With no apologies to those credit card people, don't leave home without them:

- A topographic **map** of the area.
- A **compass**, and the ability to use it in conjunction with the map. While they're excellent aids to navigation, portable GPS units are no substitute for a compass that does not require batteries or satellite reception.
- **Extra clothing**, which should consist of a top and bottom insulating layer and a waterproof and windproof top layer. A hat or cap is absolutely essential; mountaineers will tell you that when your feet are cold, put on your hat. It works.
- To avoid grazing on your **extra food**, try to pick something you would eat only if you were starving, like freeze-dried turnips or

breakfast bars that taste like pressed sawdust. Keep a box of energy bars always handy in the cupboard or car.

- Carry a **flashlight** with extra batteries and bulbs or a headlamp, which allows you to swat at the moths that fly into the light without dropping the bloody flashlight. Many of these lights have spare bulbs built-in. Lithium batteries, though more expensive, make excellent spares because their shelf-life is longer than yours.

- You can buy excellent **first-aid kits** that are already assembled. The type of injury, however, that is likely to incapacitate a day hiker may be different from one suffered by a backpacker. If your first aid kit doesn't include wraps for sprains, add an ankle support, and be sure you have some kind of blister treatment.

- **Matches** in a waterproof case are recommended over butane lighters, as both altitude and temperature can affect a lighter's performance.

- Candles work well as a **fire starter**, along with a variety of light-weight commercial products.

- A **pocket knife** is an indispensable tool.

- **Sunglasses** and sunscreen are useful, especially at high altitudes.

In addition to these items, most day hikers never hit the trail without toting some toilet paper in a plastic bag and perhaps some type of bug repellent on summer hikes. A loud emergency whistle is a lightweight addition. A small, insulating "space blanket" makes a nice lunch tablecloth—and could save your life if you have to spend the night. Binoculars are worth their weight simply for watching wildlife, and might help find your route if you become lost. Consider, too, a walking stick of some variety; it can take the stress off your knees on steep downhills, help steady you while crossing streams, and serve a wide variety of other useful purposes, such as a support post for a portable lean-to should you need emergency shelter.

Water

Dehydration is one of the most common ailments that day hikers face. No one should head out on the trail without at least one liter of clean water per person.

You'll find plenty of opportunities to refill your water bottle on most of the hikes outlined in this book. In cases where creek crossings are scarce or obtaining water might be a problem, it will be mentioned in the trail description.

Treat all water in the wilderness as if it were contaminated. The most worrisome problem might be a little critter called *Giardia lamblia,* which can give you a case of the trots that you'll never forget. The most noticeable symptom of giardiasis is "explosive diarrhea." Need you know more? Probably not.

Thankfully, there is an easy way to assure that the water you take from mountain streams and lakes is safe to drink. When used properly, filter pumps eliminate at least 99.9 percent of *giardia* and other dangerous organisms from the water. A recent and far more convenient addition to filter pumps, especially for day hikers, are the relatively inexpensive water bottles equipped with their own filters. You simply fill the bottle from the stream (taking extreme care not to contaminate the mouthpiece or drinking cap), drop the filter into place and screw on the top, and you're ready to drink filtered water. Conversely, many veteran hikers still choose to forego all this gadgetry and use the old-fashioned method: iodine-tablet water treatments, which come in tablets or crystals. The taste might be objectionable to some, but it's a guaranteed way to kill giardia and other water-borne bugs—something a filter, especially an improperly used or maintained one, is not.

Weather

In any mountains, weather can change rapidly and with little warning. On most any alpine hike in the fall, you can get snowed upon, rained upon, sleeted upon, blown around, and finally sunburned—all in the span of a day. Hikers in Washington's mountains have frozen to death in July and drowned in the afternoon while fording flood-filled rivers that were shallow in the morning. Mother Nature is most often a friendly, generous old lady who bakes cookies and bread for you, but when you least expect it she puts on a goalie's mask and whacks at you with an icicle or lightning bolt. Rain, wind, and exposure can combine forces to produce hypothermia in no time in Washington's Cascades, particularly in alpine areas, where it's always a good idea to carry waterproof, windproof gear—no matter how nice the weather looks when you depart. Wind chill and hypothermia kill far more people in Washington's Cascades than any other hazard.

In the specific case of Rainier, add to this menace unexpected snowstorms and other natural not-niceties. It's been said so often that it approaches cliché, but it's true: The mountain is such a giant physical presence, it literally creates its own climate. "Winter" as most people would normally define it lasts eight or nine months at Rainier. Many trails can be hiked only in a short summer season that lasts from July through October. Even then, bad weather can strike, especially on alpine trails exposed to the elements, which is the case with many of Rainier's most popular hikes.

Other unique challenges offered up by Rainier are avalanches (generally in the spring) and geologic hazards. The latter can range from volcanic events (extremely rare) to flash flooding and mudslides resulting from rapidly melting glaciers (also rare, but always a danger). All of that glacial ice up above makes Rainier an unstable mass of rock and water, some of which is bound to come down rapidly and unpredictably. (An example was at Van Trump Creek, where a huge muddy-debris flow—the result of a long, hot spell melting a glacier—menaced hikers on the popular Comet Falls trail in the late summer of 2001.) Hiking through volcanic creek drainages, especially during protracted hot spells, calls for extra caution: If you hear what sounds like a dozen freight trains booming down a canyon toward you, don't do what may come naturally by turning and running downstream. Head for high ground and wait it out. It's also worth remembering that, on warm days, the tiny, trickling stream you hopped over in the morning might become a raging gusher by the time you return in the afternoon.

The bottom line: On Mount Rainier, even more so than in other Cascade and Olympic mountain destinations, good planning and preparation are vital. Consult with rangers about weather and trail conditions before you leave. Tell someone where you're going. Don't take on a hike you're not mentally or physically equipped to handle. In other words, use common sense.

Flora & Fauna

For the most part, the animals and plants of Mount Rainier are benign. The most common danger might be an encounter with poison oak, stinging nettles, or, in rare instances, a black bear or a cougar.

Day hikers needn't fear black bears, but should realize these are wild animals that can cause serious injury if provoked. While there are few (if any) grizzly bears to worry about, research indicates that a black bear attack, though extremely rare, may more often lead to a fatality. A greater potential danger might be from cougars. Encounters between humans and cougars are believed to be increasing throughout Washington State, but you probably will never see one on the trail.

If you do encounter a bear or cougar, heed the following advice from the Department of Fish and Wildlife:

Bear: Give the bear plenty of room to get away. Never get between a cub and its mother. Avoid eye contact but speak softly to the bear while backing away from it. Try not to show fear and don't turn your back on a bear. If you can't get away from it, clap your hands or yell in an effort to scare it away. If the bear becomes aggressive, fight back using anything at your disposal. Should the attack continue, curl up in a ball or lay down on your stomach and play dead.

Cougar: Don't take your eyes off the cougar. Make yourself appear big by raising your arms above your head, open your jacket if you're wearing one, and wave a stick above your head. If the cougar approaches, yell and throw rocks, sticks, anything you can get your hands on. In the event of an attack, fight back aggressively.

Less dangerous, but more common hazards to day hikers include stinging and biting pests like yellow jackets, particularly in late summer and early autumn, and black flies, mosquitoes, and deer flies. Liberal doses of insect repellent (those with at least some percentage of the chemical "DEET" are most effective) can take care of the mosquitoes and deer flies, but probably won't keep those pesky yellow jackets away.

Poison oak and ivy grow in some areas of the Cascades, mostly in sunny, dry areas. A more common plant pest is stinging nettle, which grows in profusion along many trails but is easily avoided if you recognize it in time.

None of this, of course, should be construed as discouragement. We've been hiking in Rainier for a lifetime, and have yet to get lost in a snowstorm, be menaced by wild animals, attacked by killer bees, or swept away in a glacial runoff. So tighten your bootlaces, shoulder that pack, and get out on one of the hikes that follow.

Etiquette/Ethics

To protect this wonderful landscape so that users in future generations can enjoy it just as much as you, please follow a few simple rules. Stay on established trails, don't cut switchbacks, and stay off sensitive areas. Leave no trace, pack out your trash, and respect other trail users. And because you're having such a great time using Washington's trails, why not volunteer your services by lending a hand on a trail building or repair project?

Happy trails!

LONGMIRE/COUGAR ROCK

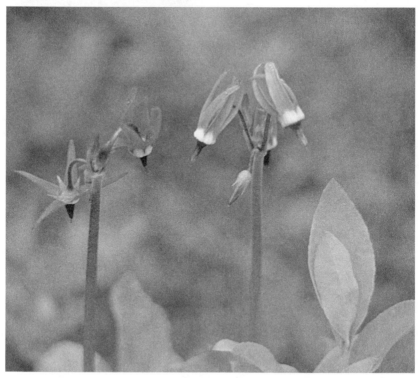

A marmot suns itself (top). Shootingstar is one of Rainier's most delicate summer wildflowers (above).

1. Kautz Creek/Indian Henry's Hunting Ground

RATING	🧍🧍🧍
DISTANCE	2.0 miles round-trip to Kautz Creek crossing/11.5 miles round-trip to Indian Henry's Hunting Ground
HIKING TIME	1.0 hour/6.0 hours
ELEVATION GAIN	250 feet/3,200 feet
HIGH POINT	2,469 feet/5,600 feet
DIFFICULTY LEVEL	Easy/Difficult
BEST SEASON	June to November/July to September; first mile of trail is snow-free much of the year; upper portions summers only
PERMITS/CONTACT	Entrance fee; no day-hiking passes required; Longmire Wilderness Information Center, (360) 569-4453
MAPS	Green Trails No. 269, Mount Rainier West; USGS Wahpenayo Peak and Mount Rainier West
TRAIL NOTES	No dogs or bikes; first mile very kid-friendly

The Hike

This is a short, pleasant day hike through a forest recovering from a glacial flow on Kautz Creek, or a full day's major ascent to one of Rainier's most memorable wildflower meadow parklands.

Getting There

From the park's Nisqually Entrance on Highway 706, drive about 3 miles toward Longmire on the Longmire–Paradise Road to the large, well-marked Kautz Creek Picnic Area on the right (south) side of the road, elevation 2,400 feet. The path begins across the road from the parking lot.

The Trail

This is two hikes in one: The first mile of the trail is an uncommonly easy stroll through a forest area recovering from a massive, muddy outburst from the Kautz Glacier, which destroyed much of the old forest here in 1947. The stream changed paths completely again during violent flooding in 2006; see the interpretive sign along the river near the trailhead. But most of the trail survived intact. The path climbs a gentle mile to a footlog crossing Kautz Creek in an area where the stream's broad, gravelly channel affords plenty of room to stretch out and down that sandwich you packed along. Bring your camera: The Mountain (assuming clear weather, which you probably shouldn't) will be beaming at you from the north. (Winter walkers should note that this portion of the trail also has become a popular winter snowshoe route.)

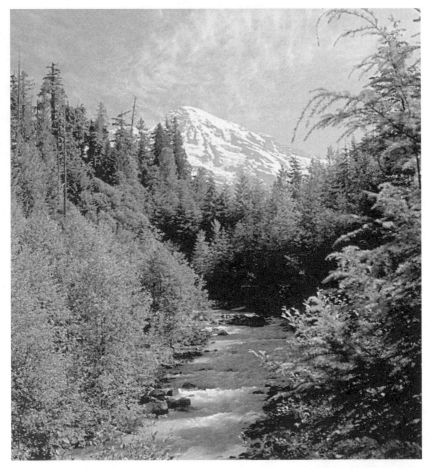

The lower portions of the Kautz Creek Trail are a great family walk; the upper parts, a challenging ascent.

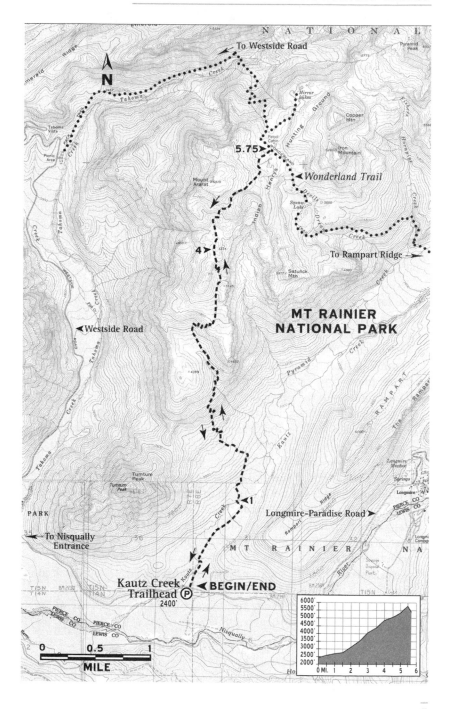

If you're up for much more adventure, though, keep on going. Assuming the footlog has not been washed out by the creek—which can be as cranky as your spouse on tax day—cross the water and get ready to climb. From here, the trail gets narrower, slicker, and, from about the 2.0-mile mark on, much, much, much steeper, switching back through a dark, lush, gorgeous old-growth forest. The grade doesn't let up until about 4.0 miles, when Rainier and surrounding peaks such as 6,010-foot Mount Ararat (on the left) and 5,577-foot Satulick Mountain (on the right) come into view.

After topping out in Indian Henry's splendid alpine meadows at 5,600 feet and 5.0 miles, you'll actually drop about 600 vertical feet over the final 0.75 mile to a junction with the Wonderland Trail and a nearby backcountry patrol cabin.

Going Farther

If your legs are still up for it after the climb, turn left at the Wonderland Trail junction and proceed about a quarter mile through the large meadow to the Mirror Lakes Trail, which leads an additional three-fourths mile and about 100 vertical feet up to a tiny set of lakes below the twin peaks of Iron and Copper Mountains. The picturesque Mirror Lake reflection of Rainier and 6,937-foot Pyramid Peak to the northeast was documented in a famous Asahel Curtis photograph reproduced on a 1934 U.S. postage stamp—ask your granddad if he remembers.

For strong hikers, another option from the Kautz Creek/Wonderland Trail junction is to continue west on the Wonderland and Tahoma Creek Trails for a one-way shuttle hike of 11 miles from the Kautz Creek Picnic Area to the West Side Road. Note that the Tahoma Creek Trail—in days of yore, by far the easiest access to Indian Henry's—is no longer maintained by the park, and can be difficult to negotiate under good conditions and downright dangerous under bad (high water) ones. And it's about a mile-long walk from the Tahoma Creek trailhead to your pickup point, the washout closure 3.3 miles up the West Side Road.

Also, hikers turning east on the Wonderland Trail from back at the Kautz Creek junction can complete a one-way through hike to Longmire via Rampart Ridge for a total of 12 miles (see Hike 4).

2. Twin Firs Loop

RATING	🥾🥾🥾
DISTANCE	0.5-mile loop
HIKING TIME	20 minutes
ELEVATION GAIN	Minimal
HIGH POINT	2,500 feet
DIFFICULTY LEVEL	Easy
BEST SEASON	May to November; accessible much of the year, except when snow levels dip below 2,500 feet
PERMITS/CONTACT	Entrance fee; no day-hiking passes required; Longmire Wilderness Information Center, (360) 569-4453
MAPS	Green Trails No. 301, Randle; USGS Mount Rainier West; but note that these and most other topographic maps do not show this trail
TRAIL NOTES	No dogs or bikes; made for kids

The Hike

Enjoy a short, easy, little-known trail offering a grand introduction to the giant old-growth Douglas fir and western red cedars found throughout Mount Rainier National Park. This is one of the first leg-stretcher hikes you'll encounter entering the park from the Nisqually Entrance.

The Twin Firs Loop is a grand place to get close to large Douglas firs.

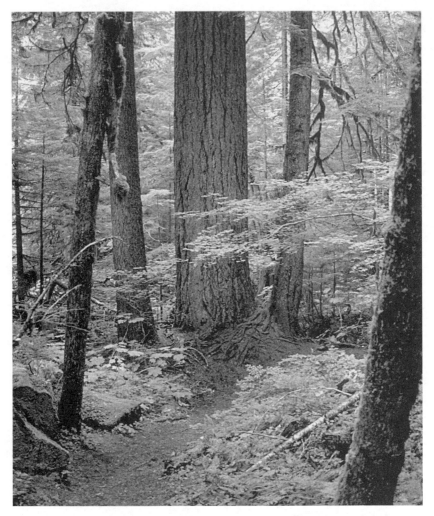

Old-growth forest provides a welcome respite in any weather.

Getting There

From the park's Nisqually Entrance on Highway 706, drive about 4 miles (0.9 mile beyond the Kautz Creek trailhead) to a pullout and visible interpretive sign on the left (north) side of the road. From Longmire, look for the trailhead about 2 miles west on the right side of the road. The trailhead, elevation 2,465 feet, is not marked by a sign, but interpretive displays mark the spot.

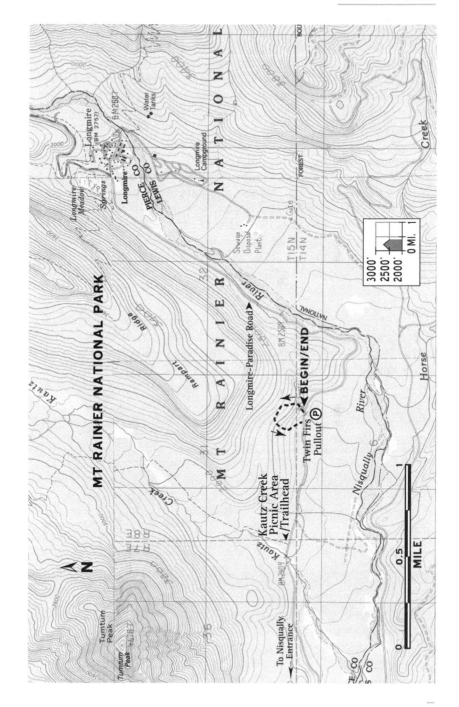

The Trail

Gung-ho mileage burners, keep right on going. Tree huggers? Step right up. The Twin Firs Loop is, quite simply, one of the more peaceful, beautiful—and unknown—nature trails on the south side of Mount Rainier National Park. (We've been visiting the park for three decades, but didn't discover this trail until we got around to compiling this guide.) Kids and the creaky kneed will love this walk. If they don't, make them do it over and over again—with you acting as old-growth-forest interpreter—until they do.

From the easy-to-miss trailhead, pull off the road and stretch your road-weary legs in the best way possible: beneath some truly stunning, behemoth Douglas firs and western red cedars. These are some of the largest you're likely to see near a road in the park, with the exception of the much more crowded Grove of the Patriarchs Trail near Ohanapecosh (Hike 24). From its outset, this delightful trail bounces along, slightly uphill, between massive old-growth trees—a perfect example of the "terminal forest" that rings The Mountain.

Unlike most trails in the park, this one is snow-free for much of the year. It's a great fresh-air outing for lodgers at the National Park Inn at Longmire, and can be combined with the first mile of the Kautz Creek Trail (Hike 2) and/or the Trail of the Shadows (Hike 3) walk at Longmire for a fine morning or afternoon of stress-free forest strolling.

3. Trail of the Shadows

RATING	
DISTANCE	0.75-mile loop
HIKING TIME	30 minutes
ELEVATION GAIN	55 feet
HIGH POINT	2,805 feet
DIFFICULTY LEVEL	Easy
BEST SEASON	June to November; accessible much of the year, except when snow levels dip below 2,750 feet
PERMITS/CONTACT	Entrance fee; no day-hiking passes required; Longmire Wilderness Information Center, (360) 569-4453
MAPS	Green Trails No. 269, Mount Rainier West; USGS Mount Rainier West
TRAIL NOTES	No dogs or bikes; very kid-friendly; first 0.25 mile is barrier-free

The Hike

Follow this easy nature trail through a meadow at Longmire that has an interesting history involving the area's first white settlers.

Longmire Meadows offers a spectacular view of Rainier.

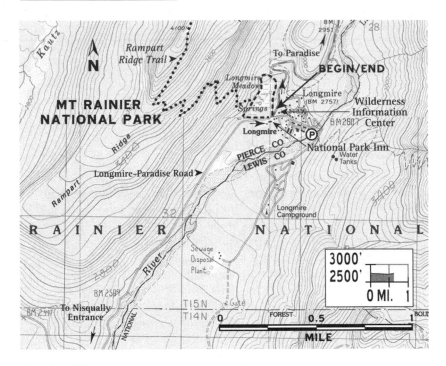

Getting There

From the park's Nisqually Entrance on Highway 706, proceed 6 miles to Longmire and park in the lot behind the National Park Inn, elevation 2,750 feet. The trail begins directly across the Longmire–Paradise Road from the National Park Inn.

The Trail

One of the most popular interpretive trails in the park, the Trail of the Shadows is, as its name implies, a pleasant, shady walk around Longmire Meadow, part of an original homestead claim by the James Longmire family. Longmire, in many ways, was most responsible for the tourist boom at Rainier. On his way to the summit in 1883, he happened upon this meadow and its bubbling mineral springs, which he was marketing to visitors a year later as a source of healing powers (the water reportedly was much warmer then).

The Shadows loop, designed to be walked counterclockwise, is dotted with signs that tell the story of Longmire's establishment here, which eventually included a hotel and other amenities (a printed trail guide is available at the trailhead). The path passes by two mineral springs and an 1888 homestead cabin built by Longmire's son.

This is a pleasant walk all year. In summer, the short spur trail leading to the center of the meadow makes a sublime Mount Rainier photo spot. In October, low vegetation bursts forth with color in Longmire Meadows. Even in the winter, this loop gets plenty of use: It's a good standby, low-elevation walk for those days when the upper mountain is socked in; when snow levels plummet, it makes a grand winter snowshoe or cross-country ski route; or just a stroll through the snowy meadows while you're waiting for snowplows to clear the road to Paradise early on those frosty winter weekend mornings.

Going Farther

The Rampart Ridge Trail connects on the west side of this loop (see Hike 4).

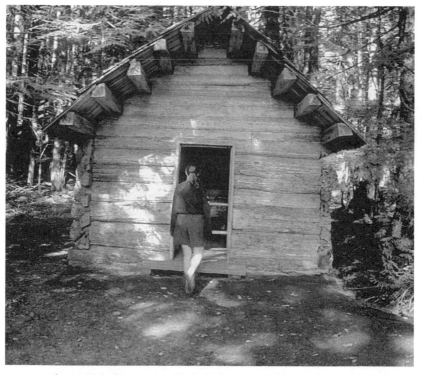

An 1888 homestead cabin built by a son of James Longmire.

4. Rampart Ridge Loop

RATING	
DISTANCE	4.8-mile loop
HIKING TIME	2.5 hours
ELEVATION GAIN	1,300 feet
HIGH POINT	4,080 feet
DIFFICULTY LEVEL	Moderate
BEST SEASON	September to October; accessible June to October
PERMITS/CONTACT	Entrance fee; no day-hiking passes required; Longmire Wilderness Information Center, (360) 569-4453
MAPS	Green Trails No. 269, Mount Rainier West; USGS Mount Rainier West
TRAIL NOTES	No dogs or bikes; okay for kids, but they might get bored

The Hike

This fairly steep, mostly forested, low-elevation loop on a prominent ridge above the Longmire area serves as a good early season or foul-weather alternative to alpine hikes.

Vine maples soak up available light in a forest of old firs.

Getting There

From the park's Nisqually Entrance on Highway 706, proceed 6 miles to Longmire and park in the lot behind the National Park Inn, elevation 2,750 feet. The trail begins on the Trail of the Shadows (Hike 3), directly across the main road from the National Park Inn. Walk that loop clockwise (to the left) one-fourth mile to the well-signed Rampart Ridge trailhead.

The Trail

Although far from the most scenic trail in the park, the Rampart Ridge Loop nonetheless gets a heavy boot-pounding every year for one good reason: its practicality. With a high point of less than 4,100 feet, and a route that follows a mostly south-facing slope, this trail usually melts out in June, well before many other popular south-side Rainier destinations, most of which climb to 5,500 feet or above. The loop begins and ends at the Longmire complex, and you can walk it either direction. Going clockwise, however, gives you more face-first views of The Mountain, when it's visible.

Walk the Trail of the Shadows Loop (Hike 3) clockwise, or left, from its trailhead for about a quarter mile to the Rampart Ridge junction. Head up the hill through deep forest on steep switchbacks for about 1.5 miles, when the grade lessens slightly. At about 1.75 miles, watch for a view looking west toward 4,678-foot Tumtum Peak, looming over the far side of the Kautz Creek drainage. A short distance farther, follow the short spur trail to a viewpoint of Rainier, Eagle Peak, the Longmire area and a vast section of the upper Nisqually drainage.

You can turn around here and be happy with a round-trip view hike of 3.6 miles. But you've done most of the hard stuff already, so press on. The path from here flattens out and follows the ridge top northeast, right toward Rainier's summit, for more than a mile, with occasional views into the Kautz drainage on the left. At mile 3.0, turn right at the Wonderland Trail junction, and in another quarter mile stay right again at the Van Trump Park Trail junction to continue on the Wonderland Trail. It's downhill all the way home from here, a shy 2 miles through pleasant forest, across the road, and then back to Longmire. Note: Carry plenty of water. None is available on the upper part of the route.

Going Farther

Feeling your oats? Add 9.2 miles and more than 2,100 vertical feet to the hike by turning left (north) at the Wonderland Trail junction, dropping down to a crossing of Kautz Creek, and hoofing it all the way up to Indian Henry's Hunting Ground (Hike 1) to create a 14-mile round-trip. Note that if your plan is to enter Indian Henry's from this side of Rampart Ridge, the practical route is to start on the Wonderland Trail at Longmire and follow it all the way to Indian Henry's, for a strenuous, round-trip hike of 12.4 miles and a total elevation gain of about 2,600 feet.

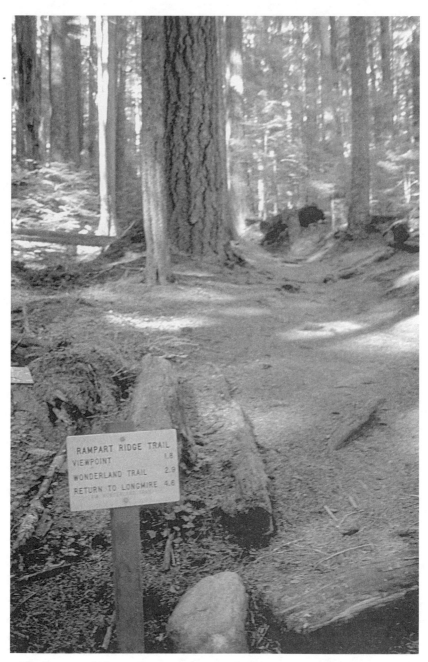

The Rampart Ridge trail connects to the Trail of the Shadows nature path.

5. Carter/Madcap Falls

RATING

DISTANCE 3.0 miles round-trip
HIKING TIME 1.5 hours
ELEVATION GAIN 535 feet
HIGH POINT 3,700 feet
DIFFICULTY LEVEL Easy
BEST SEASON July through October
PERMITS/CONTACT Entrance fee; no day-hiking passes required; Longmire Wilderness Information Center, (360) 569-4453
MAPS Green Trails No. 269, Mount Rainier West; USGS Mount Rainier West
TRAIL NOTES Kid-friendly; no dogs or bikes

The Hike

This trip is a great choice for Rainier visitors willing to trade views of The Mountain for a pleasant, uncrowded river hike with two fine waterfalls on the Paradise River. This is a good foul-weather alternative to Paradise alpine hikes. It's also the best day hike from Cougar Rock Campground, the park's most popular overnight spot.

Madcap Falls is a great destination from Cougar Rock Campground.

Getting There

From the park's Nisqually Entrance on Highway 706, proceed 6 miles to Longmire and another 2.25 miles to the wide shoulder on the right-hand side of the road near Cougar Rock Campground and Picnic Area, elevation 3,165 feet. If parking is not available along the road, continue a short distance to the Picnic Area parking lot on the right. The path begins on a footlog over the Nisqually River.

The Trail

Your new Kelty tent is pitched at Cougar Rock Campground, rain fly tauter than a drum. So now what? Lace up your boots, cross the Longmire–Paradise Road outside the campground entrance, and head upstream. This trail—actually a central section of the Paradise River/Wonderland Trail that connects Longmire and Paradise—is a perfect leg stretcher for park newcomers, or a foul-weather backup for frequent visitors who'd been hoping for clear skies up at Paradise. The cloudy-day advantage is obvious: It's tough to get lost on this route, where the Wonderland Trail crosses the chocolate-milk Nisqually on a series of footlogs before following an old service road at a gentle pace, first parallel to and then away from the raucous river.

The old road ends at about 0.4 mile, where the usually crystal-clear Paradise River announces itself noisily on the right on its way to the Nisqually. From here the path becomes a more standard trail, often following an old wooden water pipe that once fed an electrical generator below. The pace steepens slightly as a sprawling slope of crumbled rock from 5,958-foot Eagle Peak comes into view on the right (low brush puts on a stunning display of color here in the fall). At 1.2 miles, Carter Falls is seen down through the trees on the right at 3,700 feet.

Don't stop here, though. A quarter mile beyond, near the confluence of Tatoosh Creek, is less-obstructed Madcap Falls, a curious gusher in that it really slides down a broad granite step rather than tumbling like a typical falls. The gentle whitewater curtain it creates can make you dizzier than the Zip-A-Whirl at the Puyallup Fair. Turn around here and return the way you came. Or, if you've got a lunch in the pack and/or time on your hands, walk a short distance beyond to an absolutely delightful flat spot in the river just above Madcap Falls. Find broad, smooth rocks that beg

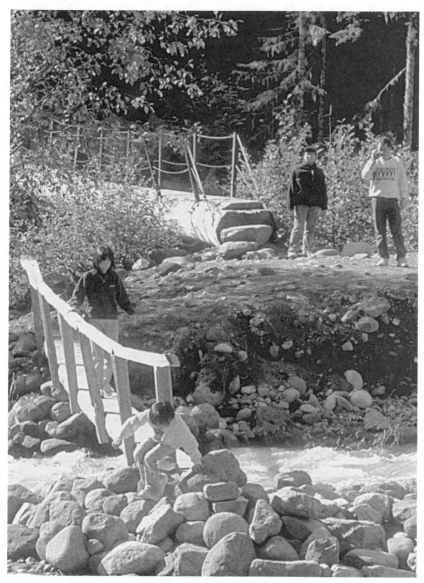

Footlogs allow passage over the milky Nisqually River.

to be napped upon and several calm, deep pools that call out to summer bathers.

Going Farther

For a longer hike, continue another 0.6 mile to Paradise River Camp, or 0.9 mile beyond that to Narada Falls, a popular roadside attraction below the Paradise area. Or, turn this trail into a 3-mile, one-way shuttle hike by starting at Narada Falls and going to Cougar Rock. Continue to Longmire for a 4.5-mile one-way hike or, alternately, begin at Longmire and walk 1.7 miles up the Wonderland Trail to the Cougar Rock trailhead. See Hike 16 for more shuttle-hiking options in this area.

6. Comet Falls/Van Trump Park

RATING	
DISTANCE	3.8 miles round-trip to Comet Falls view/6.0 miles round-trip to Van Trump Park viewpoint
HIKING TIME	2.0 hours/3.5 to 4.0 hours
ELEVATION GAIN	1,600 feet/2,200 feet
HIGH POINT	5,200 feet/5,800 feet
DIFFICULTY LEVEL	Moderately difficult/Difficult
BEST SEASON	Mid-July to mid-August; accessible mid-July through October
PERMITS/CONTACT	Entrance fee; no day-hiking passes required; Longmire Wilderness Information Center, (360) 569-4453
MAPS	Green Trails No. 269, Mount Rainier West; USGS Mount Rainier West
TRAIL NOTES	No dogs or bikes; too steep and rocky for younger kids

The Hike

Make a short, steep climb to one of the park's most popular hiking destinations—320-foot Comet Falls—with the option of going on to splendid Van Trump Park or even farther to Mildred Point, an alpine viewpoint.

Getting There

From the park's Nisqually Entrance on Highway 706, drive 6 miles to Longmire and another 4.5 miles to the Van Trump Park trailhead, at 3,600 feet, just below Christine Falls. The lot holds about twenty cars, and is often full on summer days; alternate parking is not available.

The Trail

This route has always been one of the park's most popular trails. But in the summer of 2001 it also became a showcase for just how volatile the slumbering giant volcano can be when she stirs in her sleep. The Van Trump Park Trail begins on the highway near Christine Falls and follows Van Trump Creek upward toward its

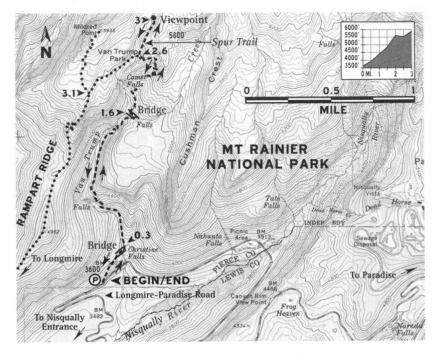

source. That pleasant little creek turned into a deluge in the warm, dry summer of 2001, when a finger of the Kautz Glacier melted rapidly, creating a mud-and-debris flow that cascaded down Van Trump Creek all the way to the Nisqually River.

Hikers at the falls that day were stunned when the water, normally a graceful, white, comet-like plume, turned into an angry, gray, chunky blast, spewing gritty mud for hundreds of yards. Nobody was hurt, thankfully. The trail was closed only temporarily. But Seattle television news anchors nearly wet their pants at the prospect of a Rainier "geological event," and those weren't the only stains: Traces of the mudflow are likely to linger on canyon walls for quite some time, serving as a healthy reminder of The Mountain's volatility.

That said, things were already getting back to normal on our last visit to this peaceful place. After crossing over upper Christine Falls about 0.3 mile into the hike, the well-worn trail climbs very steeply through the forest; take your time, keep plugging away, and tread carefully along trail portions that skirt the top of Van Trump Canyon, with the creek far below.

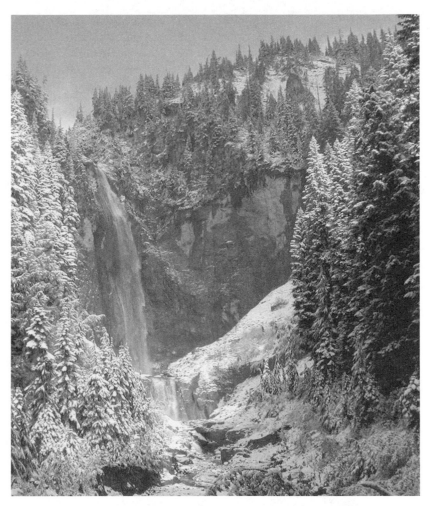

Fresh autumn snow decorates trees around Comet Falls.

At about 1.6 miles, you'll encounter a bridge over Falls Creek, which enters from the right, with a small waterfall above. Stay left on the main trail and cross the bridge; you're almost there. A short distance farther, Comet Falls comes into view on a series of steepening switchbacks. The best views of the entire, 320-foot, graduated falls are from the first several switchbacks. Snap your photos, and then continue another quarter mile to a spur trail that leads left to the base of the falls—close enough to wash your grimy face in the mist. Watch your step around the wet area below the falls.

Comet Falls is spectacular, but only the first course on this hike. Many hikers continue onward and upward, another steep three-quarter mile of switchbacks to the top of the falls and through increasingly wildflower-rich meadows. At 2.6 miles, you'll find a junction with a poorly maintained spur trail that leads just over a third of a mile north (right) through Van Trump Park to a grand viewpoint at about 5,800 feet. Bring your wildflower identification guide. A quiz will be given on the way home.

Going Farther

If it's late in the summer, the weather is good, and the footlog over Van Trump Creek just beyond the trail junction at 2.6 miles is in place (it often washes out), you can gain an even better mountain view. From the junction, continue a half mile mile south on the main trail and then take a spur trail north (right) another very steep half mile to Mildred Point. The end of the trail, 5,800 feet, is a magical spot, with stunning mountain views, an up-close look at the volatile Kautz Glacier, bountiful wildflowers, and, if you're lucky, herds of deer and klatches of mountain goats on nearby cliffs.

If you have two cars or arrange for a drop-off, you can hike one-way out to Longmire for a total of 7.3 miles excluding spur trails. To do so from Van Trump Park, continue about 4.5 miles south down Rampart Ridge via the Van Trump Park and Wonderland Trails (see Hike 4).

SOUTHWEST FOOTHILLS

Mushrooms and wildflowers are common sights on Rainier summer hikes.

7. Round Pass

RATING	🚶🚶🚶🚶
DISTANCE	7.0 miles round-trip
HIKING TIME	3.5 hours
ELEVATION GAIN	675 feet
HIGH POINT	3,550 feet
DIFFICULTY LEVEL	Easy
BEST SEASON	August to September; accessible much of the year, except when snow levels drop below 2,000 feet
PERMITS/CONTACT	Entrance fee; no day-hiking passes required; Longmire Wilderness Information Center, (360) 569-4453
MAPS	Green Trails No. 269, Mount Rainier West; USGS Mt. Wow
TRAIL NOTES	Leashed dogs okay; bikes allowed; kid-friendly

The Hike

Walk (or ride your mountain bike) up a gentle road to trailheads leading to the wild, remote side of the big mountain.

Getting There

From the park's Nisqually Entrance on Highway 706, drive 1 mile up the Longmire–Paradise Road and turn left onto the West Side Road. Follow the West Side Road 3.3 miles to the spot where a locked cable gate closes the road to the public, elevation 2,875 feet. A large parking area is located just south of the gate.

The Trail

Though in excellent condition and driven often by park staff, the West Side Road is closed to the public because of safety concerns. Park officials say mudflows and floods so frequently spit from the South Tahoma Glacier that there is a danger of private vehicles and their passengers being trapped on the wrong side of a washout. But here's the good news about the West Side Road:

* It makes a great hike for the whole family, including Fido, Tabby, or even your pet ferret (assuming all are leashed). This is one of the few places in the park where leashed pets are welcome.

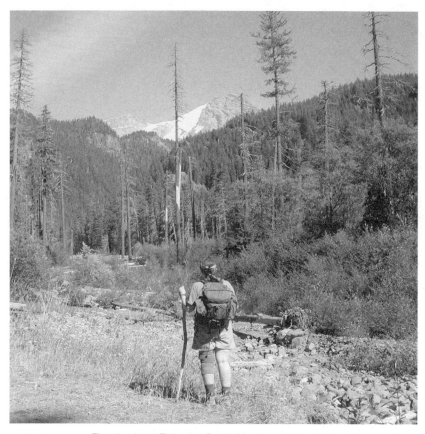

Floods along Tahoma Creek have created views
of the mountain along the West Side Road.

- You can ride a mountain bike on the road for at least 7.5 miles, one-way, to trails that climb into alpine meadows of stunning beauty.
- In winter, the road is gated just beyond its intersection with the Longmire–Paradise Road. When the snow level is below 2,000 feet, the West Side Road is an excellent family snowshoe or cross-country ski outing. When the snow level is higher, it would be difficult to find a quieter, more scenic winter walk.

The road climbs gently from the gate, first crossing a huge culvert and quarter-mile-long section of road built in 2000, after Fish Creek carved a new canyon down the middle of the old road. Just

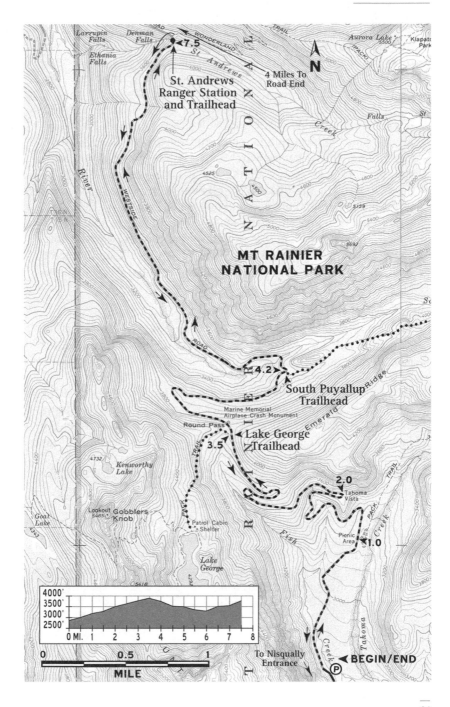

Larrupin Falls
Denman Falls
7.5
Ethania Falls

St. Andrews Ranger Station and Trailhead

4 Miles To Road End

N

Aurora Lake
Klapat Park

Falls

St

Creek

River

WEST SIDE

4525

4500

4600

4800

5139

5400

8692

MT RAINIER NATIONAL PARK

ROAD

3800

4.2

South Puyallup Trailhead

Emerald Ridge

Marine Memorial
Airplane Crash Monument

Round Pass

Lake George Trailhead

3.5

2.0

Tahoma Vista

4732

Kenworthy Lake

PACK

Goal Lake

Lookout
Gobblers
Knob

Patrol Cabin
Shelter

Picnic Area

1.0

Fish
Creek

Lake George

5418

4000'
3500'
3000'
2500'

0 MI. 1 2 3 4 5 6 7 8

0   0.5   1

MILE

To Nisqually Entrance

Tahoma
Creek

BEGIN/END

P

beyond is a spectacular view of Mount Rainier and the Sunset Amphitheater, courtesy of the last tree-killing flood and mudflow from the South Tahoma Glacier. Burn film or pixels here, because if Round Pass is your destination, this is the only photo opportunity of the mountain you'll get.

The road continues to climb gently past a picnic area 1.0 mile from the parking area. This was the site of an old auto campground and trailhead to Emerald Ridge and Indian Henry's Hunting Ground. The way now switches back and begins climbing only slightly more steeply to Tahoma Vista, 2.0 miles from the trailhead. Today, Tahoma Vista fails to live up to its name because the forest has grown and obliterated the view of Rainier.

Continue climbing along the road past two more switchbacks to a huge parking area and turnaround spot at the Lake George trailhead, 3.5 miles from the parking area. You can walk another tenth of a mile on the road to view the Marine Memorial Airplane Crash Monument.

Going Farther

Hikers seeking a longer walk can follow the Lake George Trail (Hike 8) another mile to the lake, or continue hiking the road another 0.7 mile to the South Puyallup trailhead, which leads to St. Andrews Park in a very steep 4.8 miles.

Strong, fast hikers and mountain bikers can continue past the South Puyallup trailhead for another 3.3 miles to the St. Andrews Ranger Station and trailhead. The St. Andrews Trail leads uphill to splendid Klapatche Park in 2.6 steep miles. Hikers bound for Klapatche Park would therefore hike 15 miles round-trip on the road, plus 5.2 miles on backcountry trail for a long, exhausting day hike of 20.2 miles, round-trip.

Bicyclists can continue on the road another 2 miles beyond the ranger station to Klapatche Point, where the road was closed more than three decades ago. The road originally continued 2 miles beyond Klapatche Point to the North Puyallup River, where a beautiful old stone bridge crosses the river to an auto campground. The last 2 miles of the abandoned road make a great spot to pick thimbleberries in the early autumn.

8. Lake George

RATING	
DISTANCE	8.6 miles round-trip
HIKING TIME	4.0 hours
ELEVATION GAIN	1,425 feet
HIGH POINT	4,300 feet
DIFFICULTY LEVEL	Moderate
BEST SEASON	September to October; accessible June to October
PERMITS/CONTACT	Entrance fee; no day-hiking passes required; Longmire Wilderness Information Center, (360) 569-4453
MAPS	Green Trails No. 269, Mount Rainier West; USGS Mount Wow
TRAIL NOTES	Leashed dogs okay; bikes allowed on road; kid-friendly

The Hike

Climb along a gentle road to a slightly steeper 1-mile trail leading to a clear subalpine lake. Further possibilities include a steep climb to a spectacular view of Rainier at Gobbler's Knob or a 9-mile one-way hike past Goat Lake to a trailhead outside the park at the end of Forest Road 59.

Getting There

From the park's Nisqually Entrance on Highway 706, drive 1 mile up the Longmire–Paradise Road and turn left onto the West Side Road. Follow the West Side Road 3.3 miles to the spot where a locked cable gate closes the road to the public, elevation 2,875 feet. A large parking area is located just south of the gate.

The Trail

The first 3.5 miles of this hike follow the West Side Road to Round Pass, described in Hike 7. Leashed pets and mountain bikes are welcome on the West Side Road to Round Pass, but are prohibited on the backcountry trail leading to Lake George. There's a rack at the Lake George trailhead, 3,550 feet above sea level, where you can lock your bike.

The trail climbs gently through forest for 0.9 mile to the lake. There's a patrol cabin above the shore at the northeast end of the lake and a way trail leads around the west shore. Lake George is probably a good turnaround for families with younger children.

Going Farther

It's another 1.2 miles from Lake George to Gobbler's Knob, a lookout site with an up-close-and-personal view of the west side of Rainier. You must work for the view, however, because the trail climbs 1,200 feet in that mile. If you are training for Mount Everest, that shouldn't be a problem.

Here is another option for hikers who have cars parked at the West Side Road and Goat Lake trailheads (Hike 9): Hike from either direction and meet at Gobbler's Knob for a picnic and car-key trade. The Goat Lake Trail junction is 0.2 mile below the summit of Gobbler's Knob. The Goat Lake trailhead is 3.3 miles from that junction. Heaven help the lunkhead who forgets to trade car keys. Unless you want the tougher workout and longer climb, start the one-way hike from the Goat Lake trailhead, which begins almost 2,000 feet higher than the West Side Road trailhead.

9. Goat Lake

RATING	🏃🏃🏃🏃
DISTANCE	5.0 miles round-trip
HIKING TIME	2.5 hours
ELEVATION GAIN	300 feet
HIGH POINT	4,600 feet
DIFFICULTY LEVEL	Easy
BEST SEASON	August to September; accessible June to October
PERMITS/CONTACT	USFS Northwest Forest Pass required; free USFS Wilderness Permit at trailhead; Cowlitz Valley Ranger District, (360) 497-1100
MAPS	Green Trails No. 269, Mount Rainier West; USGS Mount Wow
TRAIL NOTES	Leashed dogs okay; kid-friendly

The Hike

Take the entire family on this hike through flower-filled meadows to a clear alpine lake, with an optional climb to a lookout site with a box seat on Rainier's 50-yard line.

Getting There

Follow Highway 706 east from Ashford for 3.1 miles to Forest Road 59, on the left. You'll see a Mount Tahoma Trail Association access sign near the junction. Turn left on FR 59 and follow it 9 miles up and over a pass with a spectacular view of Rainier, to the gated road closure and trailhead, elevation 4,400 feet.

The Trail

For the first 0.1 mile, you'll share the trail with hikers bound for Glacier View (Hike 10), climbing to a junction with the Goat Lake Trail (Trail No. 248) at the crest of a 4,500-foot ridge with great peek-a-boo views of Rainier to the east. Turn right and follow Trail No. 248 as it meanders south along the crest of the ridge before descending 120 feet into Beljica Meadows.

If you've hiked in the summer, you'll soon discover why autumn might be the best time for this hike. There are enough mosquitoes

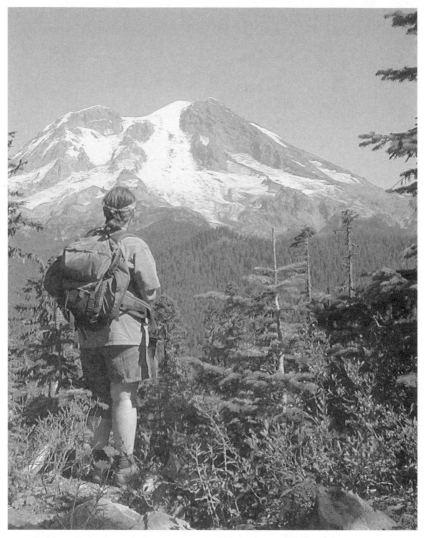

The view from the Goat Lake-Glacier View Trail.

and biting flies in the meadows and around Goat Lake to suck the South Seattle Blood Bank dry, but the poor little critters are all shivering so hard by mid-September they couldn't hit an artery with a ballistic missile.

Turn left **0.9** mile from the trailhead, at the junction with the Christine Lake Trail (Trail No. 249). The trail contours around a ridge to the north, eventually climbing in about a half mile to the high point of the hike. You'll then begin a descent, rounding a second ridge before dropping down to Goat Lake at 4,343 feet. Thus, the major part of the elevation gained on this hike is on the return trip.

Going Farther

Hikers looking for a great view of Rainier face a very strenuous climb of 850 feet in less than a mile to a 5,200-foot saddle just south of the Gobbler's Knob lookout site in Mount Rainier National Park. The trail drops slightly to a junction with the Lake George Trail, 1 mile from Goat Lake, and then climbs steeply to the lookout site. A one-way hike from Goat Lake to the West Side Road trailhead is described in Hike 8, Lake George.

10. Glacier View

RATING	🚶🚶🚶🚶
DISTANCE	5.8 miles round-trip
HIKING TIME	3.0 hours
ELEVATION GAIN	1,000 feet
HIGH POINT	5,450 feet
DIFFICULTY LEVEL	Moderate
BEST SEASON	Mid-July to mid-August; accessible July to October
PERMITS/CONTACT	USFS Northwest Forest Pass required; free USFS Wilderness Permit at trailhead; Cowlitz Valley Ranger District, (360) 497-1100
MAPS	Green Trails No. 269, Mount Rainier West; USGS Mount Wow
TRAIL NOTES	Leashed dogs okay; kid-friendly

The Hike

Walk along a forested ridge with peek-a-boo views of Rainier to the east and Mount St. Helens to the southwest. End at the airy, rocky site of a fire lookout with an unbeatable view of the west face of Tahoma.

Getting There

Follow Highway 706 east from Ashford for 3.1 miles to Forest Road 59, on the left. You'll see a Mount Tahoma Trail Association access sign near the junction. Turn left on FR 59 and follow it 9 miles up and over a pass with a spectacular view of Rainier to the gated road closure and trailhead, elevation 4,400 feet.

The Trail

This hike begins in the shade of an old forest, where you'll climb 100 feet in less than 0.1 mile to a trail junction on the ridge crest. Turn left here, on Trail No. 267, and follow it as it climbs into the sunshine of a logged area on the ridge's west side.

At **0.5** mile, you'll find an opening in the forest that frames Rainier between silver snags and likely wonder whether the view can get any better at Glacier View, your destination. It can't—but you're

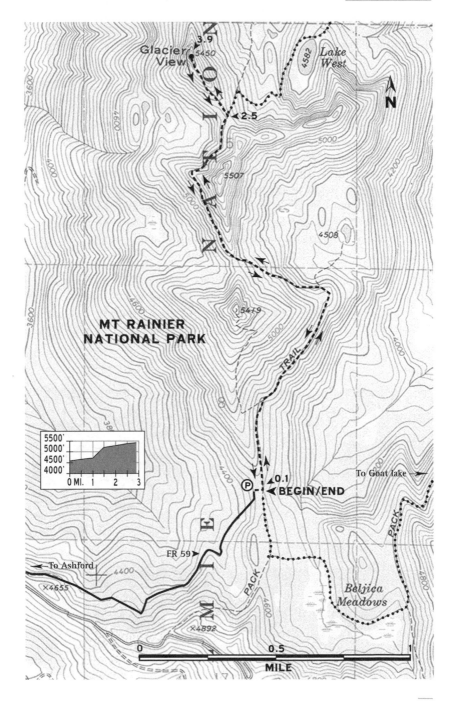

out here to put some miles on the old Vibrams, right? Continue climbing a gentle grade as the trail traverses to the east around a 5,600-foot peak and angles west back to a forested saddle, traversing under a second 5,500-foot peak. Look southwest through openings in the trees for a view of Mount St. Helens.

The trail alternately traverses steep meadows, hillside forest, and under cliffs. At 2.2 miles, you'll cross a ridge and begin descending to a saddle and trail junction at 2.6 miles. Turn left here and climb the steepest section of the trail for 0.3 mile to the old lookout site.

A flat campsite to the right of the trail, just short of the open rock summit, might be the best picnic spot. The features on Rainier best seen from here include the Sunset Amphitheater, Tahoma and Puyallup Glaciers, and Success Cleaver. The trail ends on the summit rock, unless you've brought your hang glider.

Going Farther

On a hot summer day, the cold waters of Lake West might make a refreshing stop. Return 0.3 mile to the trail junction and turn left. The trail drops steeply for 0.1 mile to a junction with the Lake Helen Trail. Keep right, here, and continue the steep 600-foot descent to the lake, another 0.7 mile.

Purple asters are a common sight on Rainier trails.

11. High Rock Lookout

RATING	
DISTANCE	3.2 miles round-trip
HIKING TIME	1.5 hours
ELEVATION GAIN	1,350 feet
HIGH POINT	5,658 feet
DIFFICULTY LEVEL	Moderately difficult
BEST SEASON	July to August; accessible June through October
PERMITS/CONTACT	USFS Northwest Forest Pass required; Cowlitz Valley Ranger District, (360) 497-1100
MAPS	Green Trails No. 301, Randle; USGS Sawtooth Ridge
TRAIL NOTES	Leashed dogs okay; no bikes; okay for kids who aren't afraid of heights

The Hike

A moderately strenuous climb brings you to an awesome cliff-dwelling fire lookout with a view of all of the big snow giants of the South and Central Cascades. There is probably no finer view of the southwest face of Mount Rainier anywhere outside of the national park.

Getting There

Follow Highway 706 east from Ashford 2.3 miles to its junction with Kernihan Road, on the right. Turn right and follow Kernihan Road across the Nisqually River, and at 1.3 miles follow the road as it curves to the left to become Skate Creek Road (Forest Road 52).

Follow Skate Creek Road for 4.7 miles to its junction with Forest Road 84. Turn right on FR 84 and follow it for 6.8 miles to its junction with Forest Road 8440. Turn right on FR 8440 and follow it 2.6 miles to Towhead Gap and the trailhead, elevation 4,300 feet. Note: At press time, FR 8440 had a short section of one-lane road.

The Trail

This is definitely not a hike for acrophobes. The final 0.3 mile of
trail climbs steep, open hillside with sheer drops of more than 500
feet on either side. If the kids go along, grab their hands on the
summit approach—even if only for your own comfort. On the plus
side, you'll be looking across the Nisqually Valley to the Kautz
Glacier and Columbia Crest. Turn around and look into St. Helen's
crater, view the glaciers on Mount Adams and in the distance on
clear days, Mount Hood.

The trail (Trail No. 266) begins by climbing along the crest of
the ridge leading to the lookout. It switches back immediately to
gain the crest of the ridge in an old logged area, and then enters
woods.

At **0.9** mile, pass beneath a minor summit on the ridge and climb
the increasingly narrow crest as the forest thins and views open
to the east and west. The trail turns to the northwest and rises 0.1
mile to the final, one-tenth-mile climb to the east, up open rock
to the lookout. Photographers prefer to take this hike early in the
morning or, better still, during the summer evening for the best

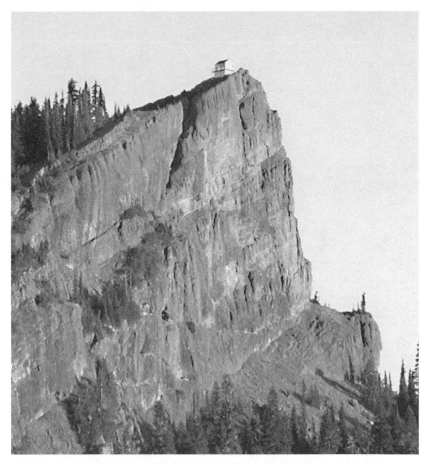

It's easy to see how High Rock Lookout got its name.

light on The Mountain. There's little point in hiking to High Rock Lookout on days when clouds shroud Rainier, unless you enjoy high places and steep cliffs.

PARADISE AREA

Crowds at Paradise sometimes can
be escaped in forests below.

12. Nisqually Vista

RATING	🚶🚶🚶🚶🚶
DISTANCE	1.2-mile loop
HIKING TIME	30 minutes to 1.0 hour
ELEVATION GAIN	About 200 feet
HIGH POINT	5,420 feet
DIFFICULTY LEVEL	Easy
BEST SEASON	Mid-July to mid-August; accessible July through October
PERMITS/CONTACT	Entrance fee; no day-hiking passes required; Paradise Visitor Center, (360) 569-6036
MAPS	Green Trails No. 270S, Paradise; USGS Mount Rainier East
TRAIL NOTES	No dogs or bikes; very kid-friendly

The Hike

Stroll along a pleasant nature trail through the sublime alpine wildflower meadows near Jackson Visitor Center at Paradise.

The Nisqually Vista Trail is the perfect one-stop Rainier hiking experience.

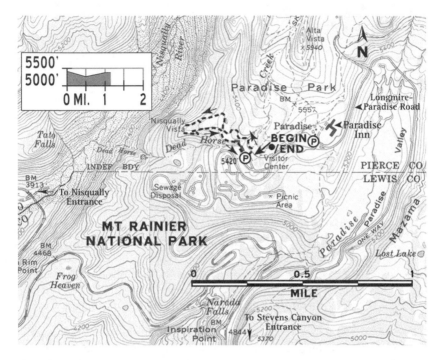

Getting There

From the park's Nisqually Entrance on Highway 706, proceed 18 miles on Longmire–Paradise Road to the main Paradise parking area, elevation 5,400 feet. The path begins in the parking loop at the west side of the main Paradise parking area (behind the old saucer-shaped visitor's center, due to be demolished in 2009). It can be reached from the new visitor center in the main parking area by following the main path up the granite steps and turning left (west) at trail junctions until you reach the marked Nisqually Vista Trail.

The Trail

If, heaven forbid, you only have a half hour to spend at Mount Rainier before that Grayline bus—or your nephew's RV—pulls out, this is probably the place to spend it. Nisqually Vista is a rolling, paved nature path that drops gently through splendid wildflower meadows to picture-postcard views of Rainier and the Nisqually Glacier, which lies literally at your feet from a viewpoint at the far end of the loop. It's an easy—although by no means flat—walk through meadows that burst into purple, white, red, yellow, and

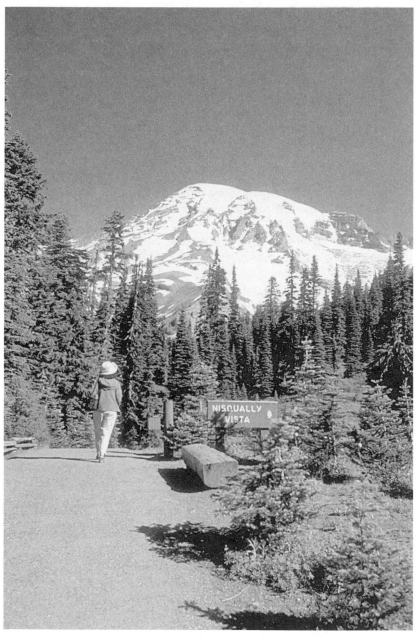

Pavement prevents erosion on the Nisqually Vista Trail and other
Paradise paths.

otherworldly scarlet when lupine, various lilies, aster, heather, bistort, and paintbrush bloom, usually from mid-July through mid-August. Even to lifelong Rainier hoofers, this is a stunning sight, and if you're here on a bright and preferably (for photography purposes) overcast day, there may be no better—certainly no more easily accessible—place on the planet to make wildflower pictures. By all means, bring the tripod.

Grab an interpretive brochure from the kiosk at the beginning of the trail and head down the hill through a fine forest of hemlock and subalpine fir, to a grand view of Rainier through the gnarled trees. You'll drop down the hill and enter a meadow with a small trickler of a stream. Stay right at the trail junction (you'll come out on the left fork on your return) for the best, in-your-face approach to Rainier.

At the center of the meadow is a small pond, Fairy Pool. In season, look close around its edges for shooting star, one of Rainier's most delicate and beautiful wildflowers. The glacier overlook is a quarter mile ahead. Spend some time at the vista and take it all in: The Nisqually Glacier looks docile from here, but it's huge and powerful. Linger long enough, and you're likely to hear it thrash and groan. The Nisqually is very active; it's been alternately creeping forward and retreating by feet and sometimes yards in recent years.

On the loop back, take in grand views of the Tatoosh Range and more lovely flower slopes. Keep your eyes peeled for blacktail deer, grouse, and other critters. Note that park naturalists offer guided walks on this path at various times in the summer; check at the Jackson Visitor Center information desk for departure times.

13. Alta Vista

RATING	🚶🚶🚶🚶
DISTANCE	1.6 miles round-trip
HIKING TIME	1.0 hour
ELEVATION GAIN	540 feet
HIGH POINT	5,950 feet
DIFFICULTY LEVEL	Moderately difficult
BEST SEASON	July to August; snow-free July to October
PERMITS/CONTACT	Entrance fee; no day-hiking passes required; Paradise Visitor Center, (360) 569-6036
MAPS	Green Trails No. 270S, Paradise; USGS Mount Rainier East
TRAIL NOTES	No dogs or bikes; mostly paved; okay for kids who like to climb

The Hike

A short, sweet, fairly steep ascent to one of the area's premium wildflower-meadow vistas.

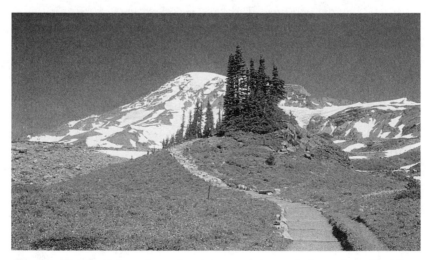

The Alta Vista path is a steep, direct approach to great views above Paradise.

Getting There

From the park's Nisqually Entrance on Highway 706, proceed 18 miles on Longmire–Paradise Road to the main Paradise parking area, elevation 5,400 feet. The route described here starts near the Jackson Visitor Center, but the trail can be accessed at various points on other trails in the lower Paradise area.

The Trail

It's a Paradise classic. No other single hike in the park, in fact, gives as quick—and, assuming good weather, as glorious—an introduction to Mother Tahoma than the Alta Vista Trail. Expect plenty of company, but don't worry about the crowds—you'll be transfixed by scenery.

Like most trails in the Paradise area, this one can be deceiving: It's mostly paved, which tends to create the impression of an easy, nature-trail stroll. But the trail is all up, up, up—and very steep in places. Take your time; there's plenty of flora, fauna, and stunning views to take in, and for most people, it gets easier as you adjust to the altitude (trust us!).

Southern views from Alta Vista stretch to Mount Adams and beyond.

The path climbs up behind the new Jackson Visitor Center, past two trail junctions, and gets thigh-crying steep as you approach a point at about a half mile that marks the bottom of the squashed-circle-shaped Alta Vista "loop." You can hike this loop portion in either direction. To take in the meadow area rising out of Edith Creek, below, take the right fork, which climbs up to a short spur leading to a junction with the Skyline Trail (see Hike 14). But if you're already running out of time or gas at the bottom of the loop, take the left fork: It's the more direct (alas, also steeper!) route to Alta Vista summit, elevation 5,940 feet. Here you can turn around and drink in the view of local meadows, the Paradise complex, the knife-ridged Tatoosh Range, and Mounts Adams and St. Helens beyond.

Believe it or not, early Paradise visitors used to take in the same view from their tents—and cars. The old Camp in the Clouds, a car camp, was located near Alta Vista back in Model-T days.

Years of hard work have created an intricate trail system around Alta Vista.

Note that you can also get to Alta Vista on a *slightly* less-steep route by turning left on the Skyline Trail about one-third mile from the trailhead and following it up the west side of Alta Vista before dropping down onto the Alta Vista Trail. This route adds only a little in the way of mileage to the hike.

Going Farther

If you're just getting warmed up at Alta Vista and starting to crave that thin air, by all means go where it's thinner: From the top of the Alta Vista Loop, join the Skyline Trail and climb another 0.6 mile and about 400 vertical feet to Glacier Vista, or beyond to Panorama Point on the upper Skyline Loop (see Hike 14).

14. Panorama Point/Skyline Loop

RATING	🚶🚶🚶🚶🚶
DISTANCE	5.5-mile loop
HIKING TIME	4.0 hours
ELEVATION GAIN	1,700 feet
HIGH POINT	7,100 feet
DIFFICULTY LEVEL	Difficult
BEST SEASON	August; accessible late July to mid-October
PERMITS/CONTACT	Entrance fee; no day-hiking passes required; Paradise Visitor Center, (360) 569-6036
MAPS	Green Trails No. 270S, Paradise; USGS Mount Rainier East
TRAIL NOTES	No dogs or bikes; not a good hike for inclement weather

The Hike

One of the highest maintained trails in the park, this challenging, stunning, high-altitude loop whisks you to—and above—all the best scenery at Paradise. It's an annual rite of passage for many Tahoma lovers.

A rock ledge appears to be a staircase to the sky from the upper Skyline Trail.

Getting There

From the park's Nisqually Entrance on Highway 706, proceed 18 miles on the Longmire–Paradise Road to the main Paradise parking area, elevation 5,400 feet. The trail starts to the west of the Paradise Ranger Station.

The Trail

On a postcard-perfect August day, we ran into a trio of older women from Puyallup up here, perched at 7,100 feet, enjoying a leisurely lunch. Members of a hiking club, they come back to Rainier to test their mettle on the Skyline Loop every year. We'll say this about them: If they can do the loop every summer and walk away smiling, they're tough and blessed all at the same time. The Skyline Loop isn't easy, and—unlike most trails at Paradise—isn't paved, at least for the crucial parts. Thus, this isn't a path for beginners—specifically all those people we see up here in sneakers summer after summer. Snow clings to the high portions of the trail well into summer and even into early fall. Sturdy hiking boots with good traction are a must, and trust us: A hiking staff or ice ax will make you feel a lot safer on the upper portions and will feel mighty good to your sore knees on the way down.

You can hike the loop either way, but we prefer a clockwise route, which gets much of the vertical over with at the beginning while you're still fresh. From the Paradise Ranger Station, follow the main (paved) path up the hill and follow signs to your left for the Skyline Trail, which climbs at a steep pace and skirts to the west (left) of Alta Vista (Hike 13). At about 1.2 miles, you'll come upon a junction with the Glacier Vista Trail. If you want a more up-close view of the Nisqually Glacier, follow the loop around; it adds only a short distance to the hike. From here, elevation 6,344 feet, continue up into the increasingly rocky, moonscape terrain, climbing at one point on a rocky ledge carved into blocky stone by trail crews.

At about 1.6 miles (6,700 feet), the Pebble Creek Trail exits up and to the left, bound for Camp Muir. Stay right on the Skyline Trail, following signs to Panorama Point, elevation 6,900 feet. From this broad vista, at about 2.0 miles, look south to the world at your feet: the glorious wildflower meadows of Paradise, marmots playing in snowfields, hundreds of hikers forming Gore-Tex ant trails from the parking lot, the stunning Tatoosh Range, and, in the far distance, the Goat Rocks, Mount Adams, and the broken, volcanic crater of Mount St. Helens. You can turn around here for

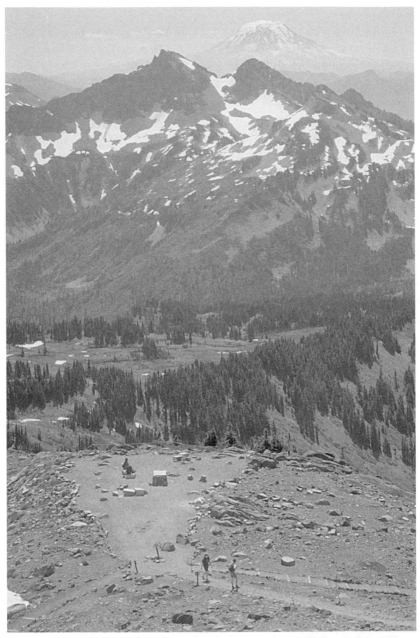

Mount Adams and the entire South Cascades are on display from the Upper Skyline Trail above Panorama Point (foreground).

a 4-mile round-trip and take the rest of the week off (if you do, at least take an alternate route, such as Alta Vista, back down); or continue on.

One trail leads due east from Panorama Point across a snowfield. This "Low Skyline" connector is a shortcut, but it's a dangerous, steep snowfield, and rangers have taken to roping it off all summer in recent years. You'll want the better view from above, anyway, so continue upward on the High Skyline Trail, which bypasses the snowfield by switching back 200 feet up a rough-and-tumble rocky slope (note the rather unsightly high-elevation outhouse below the middle switchback; don't knock it until you've sampled the view from the throne!). Come around a large volcanic rock formation, level out at an even more glorious cliff-edge vista, elevation 7,100 feet. Take a rest, get some water, and pat yourself on the tush: It's all downhill from here, cowboy. Look upward from here and see the trail of climbers coming from and going to Camp Muir on the Pebble Creek Trail.

The Skyline Trail drops quickly from here, through more loose rock and late-lingering snow, before coming to more greenery and splendid wildflowers at the Golden Gate Trail junction at 3.1 miles, 6,377 feet. You have a choice here: Bail out and take the Golden Gate Trail back to Paradise, cutting about a mile off the loop, or continue straight on the Skyline Trail. You'll drop another half mile to the Stevens/Van Trump Memorial, where the Paradise Glacier Trail (Hike 18) exits to the left at 3.7 miles. Stay right at this junction and at the next junction with the Lakes Trail along Mazama Ridge, dropping into Paradise Valley and traversing through more wildflowers, past Myrtle Falls, and back to the paved trails around Paradise.

Going Farther

The only way you can go farther from the Skyline Trail is to turn off near the loop's high point and follow the Pebble Creek Trail 0.5 mile to its end at Pebble Creek, a nice lunch spot. Or, commit to some mountaineering by following the climbers' route up the snowfields leading to Camp Muir, the overnight prep camp for Rainier summiteers (see Hike 15).

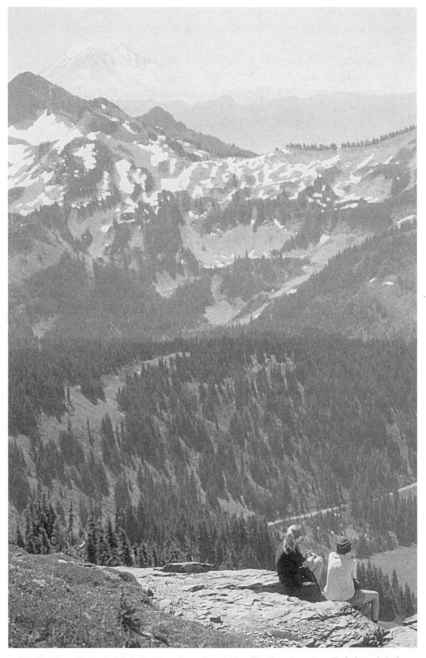

Pack a lunch and drink in the view from the Skyline Loop, a Rainier classic.

15. Camp Muir

RATING	🚶🚶🚶🚶
DISTANCE	9.0 miles round trip
HIKING TIME	8.0 to 10.0 hours
ELEVATION GAIN	4,680 feet
HIGH POINT	10,000 feet
DIFFICULTY LEVEL	Extreme
BEST SEASON	July to August; accessible mid-July through September
PERMITS/CONTACT	Entrance fee; no day-hiking passes required; Paradise Visitor Center, (360) 569-6036
MAPS	Green Trails No. 270, Mount Rainier East; USGS Mount Rainier East
TRAIL NOTES	No dogs, bikes, or fools with tennis shoes and death wishes

The Hike

A grueling, often dangerous alpine ascent from Paradise to Camp Muir, the 10,000-foot primary base camp for Mount Rainier summit expeditions.

Getting There

From the park's Nisqually Entrance on Highway 706, proceed 18 miles on Longmire–Paradise Road to the main Paradise parking area, elevation 5,400 feet. The trail starts to the west of the Paradise Ranger Station.

The Trail

It's a misnomer to call the trek to Camp Muir a "day hike." It's actually an alpine ascent that shouldn't be attempted by people without proper training and gear. We include it here to warn serious hikers to go prepared, and, frankly, to dissuade the inexperienced and ill-equipped from going at all. There's probably no better way to do this than to simply state the facts: People have become stranded and have frozen to death on this route at elevations well below Camp Muir, usually when bad weather appears from nowhere, as it often does on The Mountain.

A whiteout on the route to Muir can prove deadly even to experienced hikers. Even Rainier's backcountry rangers say finding your way down in the fog can be baffling; what you believe to be the natural fall line leading to Paradise actually leads to precipitous cliffs. The only way to be sure you're going the right way is to follow compass headings, and that's difficult with no visible landmarks. Even, clear, cloudless days can prove deadly to hikers without sturdy boots and an ice ax. Most of the upper route is across steep, open snowfields. You've been warned.

That said, for the properly conditioned and equipped (good boots, ice ax, sunscreen!), Muir remains one of the most memorable alpine ascents in Washington. It's about as close as you can get to the summit without roping up and following a guide. The first part of the journey can be made in a variety of ways through the maze of trails in lower Paradise, but most climbers follow the Skyline Trail route described in Hike 14, to its junction with the Pebble Creek Trail, elevation 6,700 feet. Here, the path climbs a series of rock steps, leveling off briefly in a half mile at Pebble Creek, a good lunch spot at 2.2 miles.

From this point on, you'll be following cairns, wands, and snow steps upward, over the Muir Snowfield. If the conditions are right, snow is deep, and steps are prekicked, it's an exhausting, albeit fairly safe, ascent. But if the surface is icy, or it's late summer and you see crevasses or surface cracks, bag it and go back. The surface you're standing on might not be safe, and unless you're roped up, you're asking for some very unpleasant crevasse-rescue training.

The climb is long and taxing; nearly 3,000 feet in 2 miles, all on snow. Plan on four hours or so from Pebble Creek. Follow the established trail through the snowfield (stay off the rock; it's fragile and dangerous), past Anvil Rock (9,584 feet) to Camp Muir, where a permanent stone bunkhouse, gear sheds, outhouses, and, typically, a small armada of mountaineering tents, are tucked between rock outcroppings. Climbers rest here for a wee-hours assault on the 14,411-foot summit via the Ingraham Glacier route. The view from the camp is stupendous—all the way to central Oregon on a clear day.

A group of climbers begin the long march to Camp Muir, the first stop on the way to Rainier's 14,411-foot summit.

16. Paradise to Narada Falls

RATING	
DISTANCE	1.6 miles one way
HIKING TIME	45 minutes
ELEVATION LOSS	900 feet
HIGH POINT	5,400 feet
DIFFICULTY LEVEL	Easy
BEST SEASON	Mid-July to mid-August; accessible mid-June through October
PERMITS/CONTACT	Entrance fee; no day-hiking passes required; Paradise Visitor Center, (360) 569-6036
MAPS	Green Trails No. 270S, Paradise; USGS Mount Rainier East
TRAIL NOTES	No dogs or bikes; a winner with kids

The Hike

This is a pleasant, all-downhill, one-way hike from Paradise through the Paradise River valley, past streamside wildflowers and numerous small waterfalls to a viewpoint overlooking majestic Narada Falls.

Getting There

From the park's Nisqually Entrance on Highway 706, proceed 18 miles on Longmire–Paradise Road to the Paradise parking area, elevation 5,400 feet. Look for the Lakes Trail trailhead at the east side of the parking area, near where the lot funnels into a one-way road through Paradise Valley.

The Trail

For a trail with multiple delights, this route gets surprisingly little use. Most people who spend a day at Paradise naturally focus on the uphill, clogging paved paths through wildflower meadows. You'll probably want to do the same, but don't overlook this fun, refreshingly cool, all-downhill walk in the opposite direction: Simply have your companions drop you at the Lakes Trail, and then arrange to meet you down the road at Narada Falls in an hour or so.

The trail drops from Paradise at a pleasant pace through the Paradise Valley, through wildflower-festooned meadows and, soon, cool forests of subalpine fir. At 0.6 mile, the Lakes Trail veers left (southeast) toward Reflection Lakes. Stay right on the Narada Falls Trail, now traveling very close to the gurgling Paradise River, one of the most beautiful streams in the park. Watch for American dippers, also known as water ouzels—small, steel-gray water birds—playing in the froth and bobbing their heads from stone perches. In a short distance, river and trail both meet the Stevens Canyon Road. Cross it, walk east across the bridge, and pick up the trail again on the other side.

From here, the path drops more quickly through cool forest, now on the east bank of the river, to the Narada Falls parking area. Note that during winter months, this same trail, marked by orange wands, is the first portion of a very popular ski and snowshoe route that continues from the Narada Falls parking lot to Reflection Lakes.

The trail ends on a closed road, near a park restroom at the Narada Falls day-use area. But before you cross the bridge to the car, pick up the paved trail across the way and proceed another 0.2 mile downhill to a viewpoint of Narada Falls, one of the most spectacular in the park. Get a picture, then walk back up to the parking area and your waiting ride.

Going Farther

If you're liking what you see, continue downstream from the Narada Falls overlook to a junction with the Wonderland Trail. Go right, toward Longmire, and follow the river just short of a mile to Paradise River Camp, continuing another half mile to Madcap and Carter Falls. From there, you can return uphill to Narada Falls, or continue another mile downhill, crossing the Nisqually River and exiting on the highway at Cougar Rock Campground. You could go even farther by continuing from the campground 1.7 miles on the Wonderland Trail to Longmire (see Hike 5). The one-way trip from Paradise to Longmire is about 7 miles, with an elevation drop of 2,800 feet.

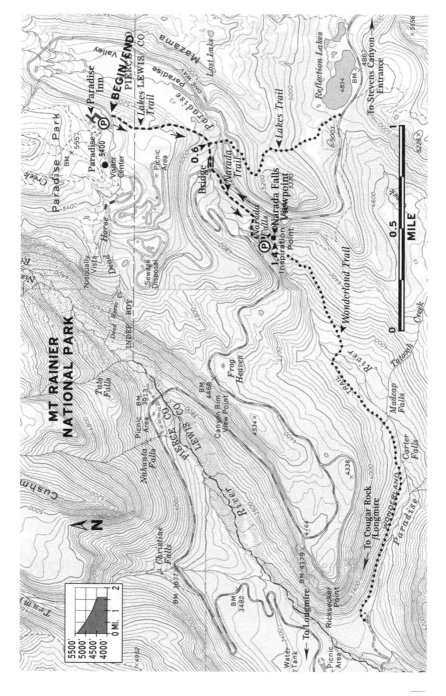

17. Upper Paradise Valley

RATING	🥾🥾🥾🥾
DISTANCE	1.8 miles round-trip
HIKING TIME	1.0 hour
ELEVATION GAIN	600 feet
HIGH POINT	5,800 feet
DIFFICULTY LEVEL	Moderate
BEST SEASON	July to August; accessible late June to October
PERMITS/CONTACT	Entrance fee; no day-hiking passes required; Paradise Visitor Center, (360) 569-6036
MAPS	Green Trails No. 270S, Paradise; USGS Mount Rainier East
TRAIL NOTES	Very kid-friendly

The Hike

Take a short, quick climb up the gurgling Paradise River from Fourth Crossing on Paradise Valley Road to Rampart Ridge, and sample some of the best views, wildflower meadows, and terrain of the Paradise area—without the crowds.

Heather blooms along the upper Paradise River are a summer highlight.

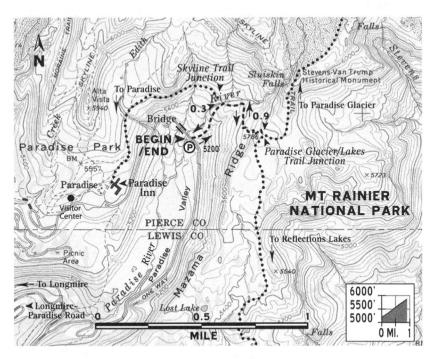

Getting There

From the park's Nisqually Entrance on Highway 706, proceed 18 miles on Longmire–Paradise Road to the main Paradise area. Continue east through the parking lot and drive downhill on the (now one-way) Paradise Valley Road. Continue about 0.75 mile to an unsigned but obvious parking area on the right side of the road, just beyond a stone bridge over the Paradise River, elevation 5,200 feet. The trailhead, marked "Fourth Crossing," is directly across the road, toward The Mountain.

The Trail

It's not listed in most guidebooks. It barely shows up on park maps. So why should you hike it? For those exact reasons. Upper Paradise Valley, shown on most maps as the Fourth Crossing Trail, is a sleeper, a little backdoor entryway into the marvelous, wild-flower-and-blue-skies extravaganza known as Paradise. We list it here because if you're like most people, you're probably arriving at Paradise on a sunny Saturday or Sunday afternoon in June, July, or August—only to find a road sign near the main parking lot bearing bad news: "Parking area full. Please proceed." Huh? You

Hikers traverse a rocky, wildflower-filled bowl below Mazama Ridge.

figured out how to strap in the kiddy car seat, crated up the dog, and fought traffic for three hours, all for a wildflower drive-by?

Fret not. A little farther down the road, where most people only venture on their way home, is Fourth Crossing, a little-used (at least in summer) connector trail between the highway and the popular Skyline Trail (see Hike 14). It follows the Paradise River—up this high, it's not really a river at all, just a delightfully exuberant stream, with plenty of waterfalls—through some of the most spectacular wildflower minimeadows in the park. And here's an added bonus: Unlike most paths departing from the Paradise parking lot, this is a real trail, with actual *dirt,* not asphalt.

The trail is a photographer's delight, offering the rare chance to photograph orange and magenta paintbrush, lupine, aster, red heather, and other wildflowers against the backdrop of rushing whitewater (Tip: cloudy days are best for photos). Watch for American dippers (small, steel-gray water birds) in the foamy water.

If you're riding on old knees, have the kids along, or don't have much time, just walk the first one-third mile up to the junction with the Skyline Trail and head back down. But if you have time, hang a right, proceed into the open bowl, and take the ascending

Feel like more? Continue up to Paradise Glacier or the Skyline Trail.

switchbacks another long half mile up to the turnaround point: the three-way junction with the Paradise Glacier and Lakes (Mazama Ridge) Trails. Mountain views from here are sublime.

If they're not quite sublime enough, just keep walking up the Paradise Glacier Trail; eventually Mounts Adams and St. Helens will pop into view.

Going Farther

There are three options for a longer hike. At the first junction with the Skyline Trail, turn left instead of right and proceed about 1.3 miles back to the Paradise parking area, where you can walk the road back to your car for a loop trip of about 2.25 miles. Or, create a longer, in-and-back day hike by following the Paradise Glacier or Lakes Trails from the trail junction at this hike's turnaround point (see Hikes 18 and 19).

18. Paradise Glacier

RATING	🚶🚶🚶🚶
DISTANCE	6.5 miles round-trip
HIKING TIME	2.5 hours
ELEVATION GAIN	1,000 feet
HIGH POINT	6,400 feet
DIFFICULTY LEVEL	Moderate
BEST SEASON	Mid-July to September; accessible July to mid-October
PERMITS/CONTACT	Entrance fee; no day-hiking passes required; Paradise Visitor Center, (360) 569-6036
MAPS	Green Trails No. 270S, Paradise; USGS Mount Rainier East
TRAIL NOTES	No dogs or bikes; okay for older or stronger kids

The Hike

One of the most popular moderate day hikes from Paradise, the Paradise Glacier Trail follows a route pioneered by early Rainier summiteers. It has since been hiked by millions of visitors who hoofed it up here to see the fabulous (and now mostly vanished) Paradise Ice Caves.

Getting There

From the park's Nisqually Entrance on Highway 706, proceed 18 miles on Longmire–Paradise Road to the Paradise parking area, elevation 5,400 feet. Look for the Skyline Trail trailhead next to the Paradise Inn, but be aware that several trails in the main Paradise complex lead to the Skyline Trail. If the Paradise parking area is full, this hike can be started from the Fourth Crossing trailhead, 0.75 mile east of Paradise on Paradise Valley Road, where parking is usually available (see Hike 17).

The Trail

More than a few old ghosts linger along this route. The Paradise Glacier Trail is actually an extension of one leg of the popular Skyline Loop (Hike 14) to a permanent snowfield high on Mount

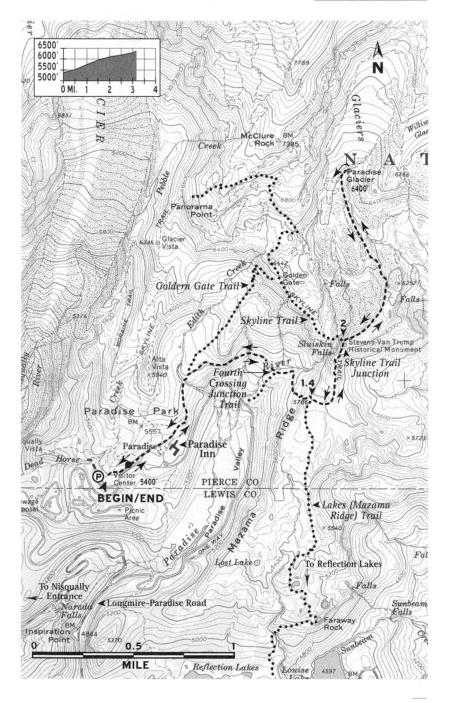

Rainier. The trail roughly follows the route chosen by early mountaineers Hazard Stevens and Philemon Van Trump, the climbers widely credited with The Mountain's first official ascent in 1870 (whether they were the first to the "true" summit is a matter of continuing debate). In midsummer, stunning fields of lilies, lupine, paintbrush, heather, bear grass, and other wildflowers blanket slopes above and below the path. Views of surrounding peaks are spectacular.

From the main Paradise trail complex, follow any of the myriad paths east to the Skyline Trail, rising steadily to a nice photo opportunity at Myrtle Falls in 0.4 mile. Then traverse gently about 300 feet downhill to the Paradise River and the Fourth Crossing Trail junction (see Hike 17). From here, the path climbs gentle switchbacks to the top of Mazama Ridge and a junction with the Lakes (Mazama Ridge) Trail at about 1.4 miles. Stay left (north) and follow the ridgeline up, checking your rear-view mirror for views of Mount Adams, until you come upon the large stone monument to the aforementioned Stevens and Van Trump (as well as their native guide, Sluiskin), who reportedly parked their base camp here, about 2.0 miles from where you parked your Lincoln Navigator.

The Skyline Trail joins near here; stay right and head up through the moonscape-like, dusty terrain typical of Rainier above 6,000 feet. You'll follow an old moraine of the Paradise Glacier for about a mile through barren and exposed terrain—beware bad weather here—to the glacier itself, now essentially a permanent snowfield quite popular with early- and late-season backcountry skiers and snowboarders.

Cairn markers still lead the way to the former site of the Paradise Ice Caves, one of Rainier's leading attractions until glacial retreat claimed them. Some wind-carved ice caves do still present themselves here on occasion: Don't enter them unless you know what you're doing, which most of us don't. The view behind you of Mount Adams, Mount St. Helens, the Goat Rocks, and the Tatoosh Range is reward enough for this climb.

Note: Upper portions of the trail remain snow covered until late summer; wear sturdy hiking boots and stay on the marked trail.

Going Farther

You can return to Paradise via the Skyline or Golden Gate Trails for a longer hike with more elevation gain (see Hike 14).

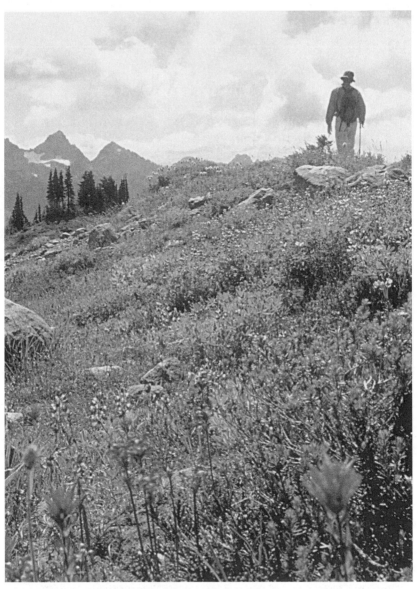

Wildflowers and views of the Tatoosh Range are highlights of the
Paradise Glacier Trail.

19. High Lakes Loop

RATING 👣👣👣👣
DISTANCE 3-mile loop
HIKING TIME 2.0 hours
ELEVATION GAIN 600 feet
HIGH POINT 5,500 feet
DIFFICULTY LEVEL Moderate
BEST SEASON Mid-July to mid-August; accessible late June through October
PERMITS/CONTACT Entrance fee; no day-hiking passes required; Paradise Visitor Center, (360) 569-6036
MAPS Green Trails No. 270S, Paradise; USGS Mount Rainier East
TRAIL NOTES No dogs or bikes; okay for strong kids

The Hike

A short, pleasant, moderate loop with great views, ample wild-flowers, and abundant wildlife takes you by the shores of gorgeous alpine lakes.

Getting There

From the park's Nisqually Entrance on Highway 706, proceed 15.6 miles on Longmire–Paradise Road to the Stevens Canyon turnoff. Turn right and follow Stevens Canyon Road 1.7 miles to the long parking area along Reflection Lakes, elevation 4,865 feet. The loop begins on the Wonderland Trail at either end of the parking lot.

The Trail

Here's a grand way to sample all the alpine delights of the Paradise area without fighting the Paradise crowds. Make no mistake: Reflection Lakes is probably number two on Rainier's day-use hit parade, so you still might need to get here early on a summer weekend. But once you're out of the parking lot, you're not liable to run into nearly as many gapers from Nebraska out for a day on the trail.

You can walk this loop, which combines three separate trails, in either direction (and you can walk a longer version of it from Paradise; see "Going Farther" below). But we like to start on the west side of the parking lot, hiking in a clockwise direction and saving the big view from Faraway Rock for the end.

Begin on the Wonderland Trail (mileages indicated here are from the center of the parking lot). In a short distance, go right on the Lakes Trail and head up through a wet, meadowy area to a junction with the High Lakes Trail at **0.75** mile and 5,100 feet. Turn right (east) and traverse about 1.25 miles across pleasantly flat trail through a mixed forested area, with occasional views of Rainier and the Tatoosh Range, to a junction with the Lakes (Mazama Ridge) Trail at **2.0** miles and 5,300 feet. Turn right, and head back downhill, stopping for a look at Artist Pool (a small tarn) and then at Faraway Rock to take in the precipitous, cliff-edge view of Lake Louise, Reflection Lakes, the Tatoosh Range, and much of Stevens Canyon. Stay away from the edge: It's about 500 feet down.

The trail back down to the car is gorgeous, with ample wildflowers and wild huckleberries in season. Keep your eyes peeled for blacktail deer or even a rare black bear. At about **2.6** miles, meet up again with the Wonderland Trail. Stay right and follow it a short distance back to the parking area.

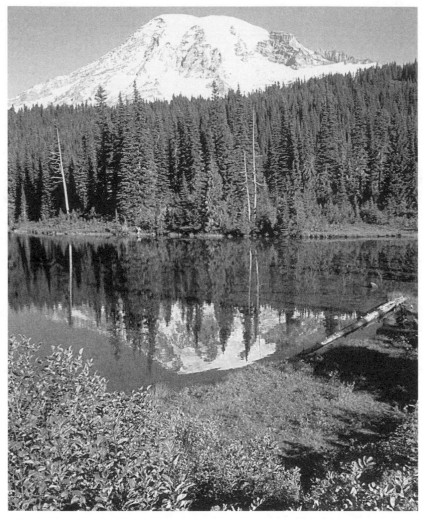

Aptly named Reflection Lake greets hikers completing the High Lakes Loop.

Going Farther

You can make a loop of about 6 miles by hiking the Lakes Trail north from Reflection Lakes all the way up Mazama Ridge to the Skyline Trail, walking east to Paradise, and then south back to Reflection Lakes via the western portion of the Lakes Trail.

20. Pinnacle Saddle

RATING	🚶🚶🚶🚶
DISTANCE	2.6 miles round-trip
HIKING TIME	2.0 hours
ELEVATION GAIN	1,055 feet
HIGH POINT	5,920 feet
DIFFICULTY LEVEL	Moderately difficult
BEST SEASON	August to September; accessible mid-July through October
PERMITS/CONTACT	Entrance fee; no day-hiking passes required; Paradise Visitor Center, (360) 569-6036
MAPS	Green Trails No. 270S, Paradise; USGS Mount Rainier East
TRAIL NOTES	No dogs or bikes; okay for strong kids

The Hike

On clear days, this is a delightful, view-rich ascent from Reflection Lakes. Climb through subalpine forest into open, rocky terrain to a grand vista of Rainier from the saddle between Pinnacle and Plummer Peaks, two crown jewels of the Tatoosh Range.

Getting There

From the park's Nisqually Entrance on Highway 706, proceed 15.6 miles on Longmire–Paradise Road to the Stevens Canyon turnoff. Turn right and follow Stevens Canyon Road 1.7 miles to the long parking area along Reflection Lakes, elevation 4,865 feet. The trail begins across Stevens Canyon Road from the center of the parking strip.

The Trail

Okay, there has to be one, single *best* view of Rainier from the south side of the park. And this is it. You'll have to sweat a little to get there, but Pinnacle Saddle is one of the most impressive day hikes in the park—a certified Do Not Miss for lovers of high alpine views.

From the Reflection Lakes parking lot, begin climbing gently through a pleasant forest, with occasional meadows dotted by pink Lewis monkeyflower and other blossoms. At about **0.5** mile, the pace

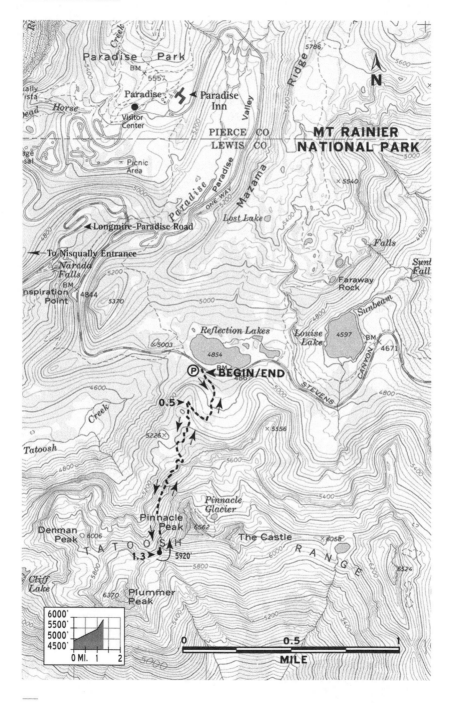

steepens. You'll cross several large boulder fields as views of Rainier, the upper Nisqually drainage, and even faraway Comet Falls begin to open up. Before you know it, you'll be rising above tree line, following a very rocky, consistently steep path through a rubble field below imposing, 6,562-foot Pinnacle Peak. Note the great rock work done over the decades here by trail crews, who have built landscape-perfect rock walls using only available materials and muscle.

It feels like a long 1.3 miles up, but the scene at the top is one of the most dramatic in the park: A narrow gap in the saddle between rocky Pinnacle and Plummer Peaks opens to sweeping views of the South Cascades, from Mount St. Helens to Mount Adams, and the Goat Rocks (themselves the remnants of an ancient, collapsed volcano). Turn around and, if it's clear, prepare to be wowed: Rainier in all her south-face glory is rarely on finer display than from right here.

Note that this is another Rainier trail where sturdy hiking boots are vital. Snow lingers on the upper portions well into the summer, and a hiking staff or ice ax can be of great aid. Also, carry plenty of water. None is available along the route after midsummer.

Going Farther

From the saddle, numerous way trails spread out east and west. The eastern path winds up toward the top of Pinnacle Peak, but quickly deteriorates into an open rock scramble. Proceeding beyond this point without climbing gear and knowledge is a dangerous gamble.

One trail to the west leads along the gorgeous parkland of the saddle to some great lunch spots with sunny, south-facing views; another climbs the ridge toward the top of Plummer Peak, where a small tarn is located. It's a fairly exposed, cliff-top route.

21. Bench and Snow Lakes

RATING	🚶🚶🚶
DISTANCE	2.6 miles round-trip
HIKING TIME	1.5 hours
ELEVATION GAIN	700 feet
HIGH POINT	4,700 feet
DIFFICULTY LEVEL	Moderate
BEST SEASON	Mid-July through September; accessible July through October
PERMITS/CONTACT	Entrance fee; no day-hiking passes required; Paradise Visitor Center, (360) 569-6036
MAPS	Green Trails No. 270S, Paradise; USGS Mount Rainier East
TRAIL NOTES	No dogs or bikes; okay for strong kids

The Hike

Enjoy rich views on this hike with plenty of up and downs and a pair of scenic alpine lakes in the shadow of Mount Rainier.

A well-worn path crosses "The Bench" on its way to Snow Lake.

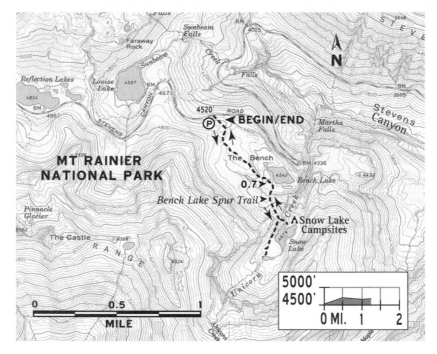

Getting There

From the park's Nisqually Entrance on Highway 706, proceed 15.6 miles on Longmire–Paradise Road to the Stevens Canyon turn-off. Turn right and follow Stevens Canyon Road 3 miles east, past Reflection Lakes and Louise Lake, to a small turnout on the right side of the road, elevation 4,520 feet. Note that the lot only holds about a dozen cars, and often is full in the summer.

The Trail

Don't be fooled by the map. Bench and Snow Lakes, twin alpine beauties in a broad expanse of meadowland with gorgeous displays of summer wildflowers and often-spectacular autumn color, lie at about the same elevation as the trailhead. But you'll do quite a bit of up and down to get there, and on warm summer days the route can be hot, the trail dusty. On the other hand, none of these things ever stopped you before, and the view from Snow Lake makes the trail, the crowds, and even the annoying black flies—which can be atrocious here in midsummer—seem bearable.

From the trailhead along Stevens Canyon Road, the trail climbs quickly up the first ridge, at times on a boardwalk installed over a particularly muddy or dusty area (depending on the weather). As you descend the far side and level out, you'll be walking on "The Bench," a broad plain with open meadows, a few old snags, and killer mountain views. At 0.7 mile, a short spur trail leads down to Bench Lake. Don't waste your time with the steep, unmaintained approach. There's not much to see at the shore, and thickets of scrubby alders and other shrubs prevent you from walking along the lake.

Snow Lake is another story. Continue another half mile, crossing a marshy area and then climbing another ridge. The lake, perched in a glacial cirque below 6,935-foot Unicorn Peak, the king of the Tatoosh Range, is a stunner, with deep, turquoise water and a fabulous view of Rainier. Expect snow to linger on the far side of the lake well into the summer. A side trail leads a quarter mile to the left, across Unicorn Creek and down to the lakeshore to two backcountry campsites that look too good to be true. They're not; with a bit of permit-reservation magic, you could come back and spend a night here. A more memorable view would be hard to find. Remember to save some energy for the trip out: about 300 feet of this hike's elevation gain comes at the end.

STEVENS CANYON/ OHANAPECOSH

The cool, damp forests of the Ohanapecosh valley can be a welcome change from alpine hikes.

22. Stevens Creek

RATING 🚶🚶

DISTANCE	1.4 miles round-trip
HIKING TIME	1.0 hour
ELEVATION GAIN	535 feet
HIGH POINT	3,100 feet
DIFFICULTY LEVEL	Moderately difficult
BEST SEASON	Anytime it's accessible, June to October
PERMITS/CONTACT	Entrance fee; no day-hiking passes required; Ohanapecosh Visitor Center, (360) 569-6046
MAPS	Green Trails No. 270, Mount Rainier East; USGS Mount Rainier East
TRAIL NOTES	No dogs or bikes; too steep for kids or creaky knees

The Hike

Make a short, steep hike downhill through a mixed forest to a unique waterfall on Stevens Creek.

Getting There

From the park's Stevens Canyon Entrance on Highway 123, drive about 10.8 miles west on Stevens Canyon Road to the Box Canyon Picnic Area (just beyond the tunnel after the Box Canyon Exhibit) on the left (south) side of the road, elevation 3,100 feet. The trail begins on the east side of the parking lot. If you're arriving from the west, the trailhead is about 8.3 miles west of the junction with the Longmire–Paradise Road.

The Trail

Stevens Creek Trail isn't flashy, but it goes someplace pretty special. On first glance, only two things stand out about this little-used connector between Stevens Canyon Road and the Wonderland Trail, far below in Stevens Canyon: the topography and the decided lack of crowds. Unlike most trails you're likely to hike in Rainier, this one drops down below 3,000 feet, through a fascinating forest of white-barked birch and other deciduous trees. Sword ferns and other greenery dot the forest floor, which is alive with fungi,

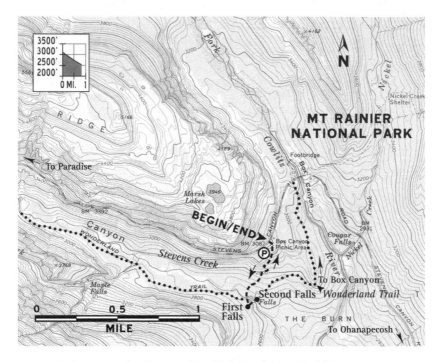

mushrooms, and other moist-climate plants you'd expect to see in a temperate rainforest or low-lying forest around Puget Sound. It's almost like walking through a terrarium; the forest is peaceful and silent until you reach **0.5** mile, when Stevens Creek becomes audible below.

When the trail reaches the dark, humid canyon floor, you'll find a short spur leading left down to a fenced overlook of a gorgeous, unnamed low-rushing falls on Stevens Creek. A short distance downstream is another falls. Continue on about a tenth of a mile to a junction with the Wonderland Trail and a bridge over Stevens Creek. The stream here is fascinating, filled with large, smooth, almost sculpted boulders. If you're like us, you'll be wishing you had more light down here to make photographs—and wishing you hadn't packed that heavy long lens. The trek back up the trail to the car is even worse than you feared on the way down. It's unmercifully steep, but mercifully short.

Going Farther

You can follow the Wonderland Trail from the Stevens Creek Bridge at the end of this hike for an additional 1.2 miles and

The falls on Stevens Creek is the only sound you're likely to hear on this hike.

400 vertical feet up to the Box Canyon interpretive site on Stevens Canyon Road. The 0.3 mile interpretive trail at Box Canyon, where the Muddy Fork of the Cowlitz River cuts through a deep gorge, is also well worth your time.

23. Cowlitz Divide

RATING	🚶🚶🚶🚶
DISTANCE	11.8 miles round-trip
HIKING TIME	6.5 hours
ELEVATION GAIN	2,850 feet
HIGH POINT	5,900 feet
DIFFICULTY LEVEL	Difficult
BEST SEASON	July to September; accessible July to October
PERMITS/CONTACT	Entrance fee; no day-hiking passes required; Ohanapecosh Visitor Center, (360) 569-6046
MAPS	Green Trails No. 270, Mount Rainier East; USGS Ohanapecosh Hot Springs
TRAIL NOTES	No dogs or bikes; not a good choice for kids

The Hike

Save this strenuous hike for a clear day to appreciate the spectacular view of Rainier and the green valley of Indian Bar. Strong hikers can continue 1.9 miles to Indian Bar—one of the most scenic backcountry camps in the park—or with a car-key exchange, can continue past Indian Bar to the Summerland trailhead, 15.5 miles one-way.

Getting There

Drive up the Stevens Canyon Road 10 miles from the park's Stevens Canyon Entrance on Highway 123 to the Box Canyon parking area, elevation 3,050 feet. The trailhead is across the road from the parking area, just east of the Box Canyon Nature Trail.

The Trail

One advantage to this serious climb is that the trail is mostly in forest shade. You'll stay relatively cool until you approach the recommended turnaround spot, a 5,900-foot knoll with a stunning view of The Mountain and of Indian Bar, 800 feet below.

Begin by climbing at a moderate grade to a footlog across Nickel Creek at 1.0 mile. Pass a large group camp on the opposite side of

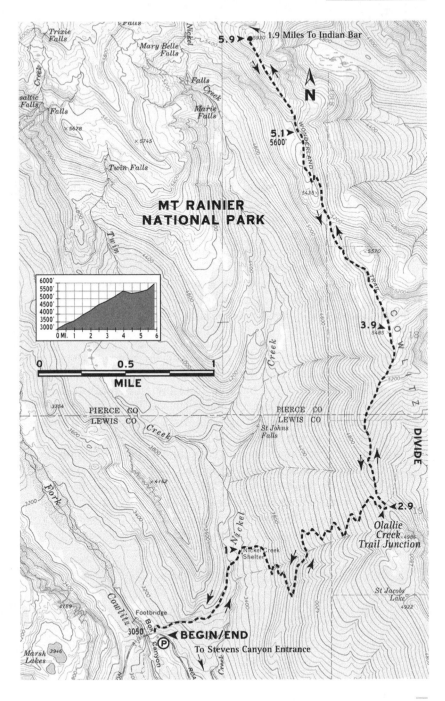

Trixie
Falls

Mary Belle
Falls

Nickel

5.9 ▶ 5930 1.9 Miles To Indian Bar

Falls

Falls
Creek

Marie
Falls

N

saltic
Falls Falls

× 5678

× 5745

5.1 ▶
5600'

Twin Falls

MT RAINIER
NATIONAL PARK

Twin

6000'
5500'
5000'
4500'
4000'
3500'
3000'
0 MI. 1 2 3 4 5 6

Creek

× 5570

3.9 ▶
5485

0   0.5   1
MILE

C
O
W
L
I
T
Z

18

PIERCE CO
LEWIS CO

3784

Creek

PIERCE CO
LEWIS CO

St Johns
Falls

D
I
V
I
D
E

× 4182

Fork

◀ 2.9

Olallie
Creek
Trail Junction

St Jacobs
Lake
4922

3200

Nickel

4189

Nickel Creek
Shelter

Cowlitz

Footbridge

3050

Box
Canyon

◀ BEGIN/END
To Stevens Canyon Entrance

Marsh
Lakes

3946

Creek

91

the creek with a minimalist food-hanging device that looks as if it were designed by the bears. The trail now climbs more steeply, crossing a Nickel Creek tributary only to switch back and recross the creek. The trail climbs steadily in switchbacks for 1.9 miles, gaining more than 1,000 feet, to Cowlitz Divide and a junction with the Olallie Creek Trail at 2.9 miles. Turn left at the junction and follow the Wonderland Trail as it climbs along the crest of Cowlitz Divide.

The trail continues through forest for another mile, climbing steeply at times over the top of a 5,400-foot summit at 3.9 miles. You'll keep climbing through thinning forest past a 5,600-foot peak on the left at 5.1 miles. The way continues up the ridge for another 0.8 mile to a wide knoll, at 5,900 feet and 5.9 miles from the trailhead.

This is a good spot for a picnic and turnaround, with views of Rainier's Ohanapecosh Glacier and Mount Tahoma. In the valley below is the infant Ohanapecosh River and fabled Indian Bar, a splendid alpine campsite and meadow. Take off your boots and let the mountain breezes cool those barking dogs.

Going Farther

From this point, the trail drops steeply into the valley, arriving at Indian Bar 7.8 miles from the trailhead. Strong hikers willing to climb the 800 vertical feet back up from Indian Bar will find the scenery well worth the extra 1.9 miles. The valley is wide and flat, wildflowers abound, and few places around the park are so well-suited for hanging out in the sunshine.

An option for marathon day-hikers with cars parked at both the Box Canyon and Summerland trailheads (Hike 33) is a one-way hike and key exchange at Indian Bar, about halfway on the 15.5-mile trek. The Summerland trailhead starts at about 3,800 feet above sea level, while the Box Canyon trailhead is at about 800 feet—but hikers from either direction must cross 6,700-foot Panhandle Gap.

24. Grove of the Patriarchs

RATING	🥾🥾🥾🥾🥾
DISTANCE	1.25 miles round-trip
HIKING TIME	45 minutes to 1.0 hour
ELEVATION GAIN	Negligible
HIGH POINT	2,200 feet
DIFFICULTY LEVEL	Easy
BEST SEASON	June through October
PERMITS/CONTACT	Entrance fee; no day-hiking passes required; Ohanapecosh Visitor Center, (360) 569-6046
MAPS	Green Trails No. 270, Mount Rainier East; USGS Chinook Pass
TRAIL NOTES	No dogs or bikes; perhaps the best kid trail in the entire park

Hiking among the Douglas fir giants on the Grove of the Patriarchs Trail.

The Hike

This is a very easy, memorable walk through a splendid old-growth forest on an island in the middle of the beautiful Ohanapecosh River.

Getting There

From the park's Stevens Canyon Entrance on Highway 123, proceed a short distance east, across the Ohanapecosh River bridge, to the trailhead parking area on the right (north) side of the road, elevation 2,200 feet. The lot, which holds about two dozen cars, is often full on summer days. Rangers do not allow parking along the road, but if you can't find a spot, don't give up: Consider parking at the nearby Laughingwater Creek trailhead on Highway 123 or

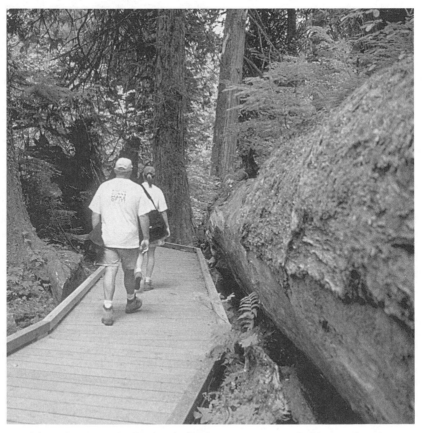

A boardwalk on the Patriarchs Trail protects roots of old-growth trees.

farther south at Ohanapecosh Campground and walking the East-side Trail upstream, past Silver Falls, to the Grove of the Patriarchs Trail (see Hike 25).

The Trail

Walking this path over the years, we've encountered people of all ages, of all races, from all different countries, and in all shapes and sizes, and all of them exhibit one common behavior: reverence. In the Grove of the Patriarchs, you don't run, you don't shout, you don't cavort or gripe. It would be like goofing off in church, which is what this grove of massive western hemlock, western red cedars, and Douglas fir is to multiple generations of Northwest nature lovers. The Grove is one of the more popular destinations in Mount Rainier National Park, and one of the more memorable stands of old-growth anywhere in the country.

The guardian of all this arboreal splendor is the Ohanapecosh River, which forms a protective ring around the small island hosting the Patriarchs, thus keeping them from fire over the centuries. The result is a stirring monument to tenacity: dozens of trees more than 25 feet in circumference—some as much as 50 feet around—and up to one thousand years old.

To get to them, walk the flat, pleasant path upstream from the always-crowded trailhead, beneath several lovely old red cedars, to a crossing of the Ohanapecosh at just less than half a mile. Walk across the steel suspension bridge—the sign says one body at a time, so on a busy day you might have to wait your turn—and follow the trail a short distance to the first really, really big tree, a contorted red cedar, on your left.

Here begins a grand addition to the trail: A raised wooden board-walk, which will carry you on a 0.3-mile loop beneath the Patriarchs. The boardwalk was two years in the making, and is one of the best user-fee-supported projects we've seen in the Northwest. Fortunately, it survived the massive 2006 floods, although the suspension bridge crossing the river to reach it was heavily damaged. The boardwalk protects the old giants' roots and bark from excessive—and damaging—tree hugging and cavorting by visitors. Take your pictures next to the massive Twin Firs, and by all means, take your time walking through here: It's a true treat, in any weather.

25. Silver Falls Loop

RATING	🚶🚶🚶🚶
DISTANCE	3-mile loop
HIKING TIME	1.5 hours
ELEVATION GAIN	330 feet
HIGH POINT	2,200 feet
DIFFICULTY LEVEL	Easy
BEST SEASON	May through October
PERMITS/CONTACT	Entrance fee; no day-hiking passes required; Ohanapecosh Visitor Center, (360) 569-6046
MAPS	Green Trails No. 270, Mount Rainier East, and No. 302, Packwood; USGS Ohanapecosh Hot Springs and Chinook Pass
TRAIL NOTES	No dogs or bikes; great hike for kids

The Hike

Take an easy walk from Ohanapecosh Campground to Silver Falls, one of the park's most impressive lower-altitude sights.

Getting There

Drive to Ohanapecosh Campground, elevation 1,870 feet, located on Highway 123 about 1.8 miles south of the Stevens Canyon Entrance to Mount Rainier National Park. The trail begins at the end of the first camping loop to your right. Drive around the loop and park in day-use spots, if available. If not, you might have to park back up the hill, at the Ohanapecosh Ranger Station, and walk a half mile back to the trailhead. (Do not, as some guidebooks suggest, park in front of the Ohanapecosh Visitor Center. Those spots have been changed to short-term parking, and you risk being towed.)

The Trail

This trail may well be responsible for what you hold in your hand. The Silver Falls Trail is one of the first Northwest hiking memories still accessible in the cluttered hard drive of this author's brain. He can vaguely remember setting off on the path with his older sister, both fitted with tiny daypacks, and returning with the feeling he'd

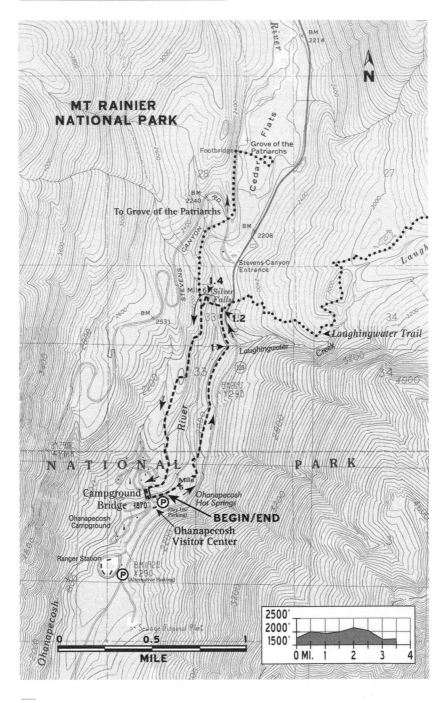

really accomplished something. More than three decades later, not much has changed: You'll still feel like you've accomplished something, no matter your age or ability. It's a popular trail, one of the first to melt out in the spring. Expect plenty of company from the sprawling campground, one of Rainier's prime overnight spots.

This path proceeds at a pleasant grade upstream, following the stunningly crystal-clear Ohanapecosh River (thanks to mostly inactive glaciers at its source, it doesn't carry the glacial flour of most Rainier rivers). At 1.0 mile, cross lovely Laughingwater Creek and reach a junction with the Laughingwater Creek Trail at 1.2 miles. Walk over a short rise to Silver Falls at 1.4 miles, one of the more impressive gushers in the park. Come in the early summer if you want to witness the really big splash. The trail crosses the river as it plunges below the falls into a steep gorge. On the far side, follow the path up to a viewpoint near the top of the falls.

You can return the way you came, but it's not much farther to complete the loop from here. Above the overlook, turn left on the Eastside Trail and stay left again where the Cowlitz Divide Trail branches off. You'll gain altitude steadily for the next three-fourths mile or so, entering a quiet, dark forest and eventually descending back to Ohanapecosh Campground on the west side of the river.

Note: If you're pressed for time and just want to see Silver Falls, you can also reach it via a short, steep hike down the Laughingwater Creek Trail, along Highway 123 north of Ohanapecosh Campground.

Going Farther

From the Eastside Trail junction above Silver Falls, you can continue north on the Eastside Trail for a long half mile, and about 250 vertical feet, along a beautiful stretch of the river to Stevens Canyon Road and the Grove of the Patriarchs Trail (Hike 24). You can combine both hikes for a satisfying round-trip of about 5.5 miles from Ohanapecosh Campground.

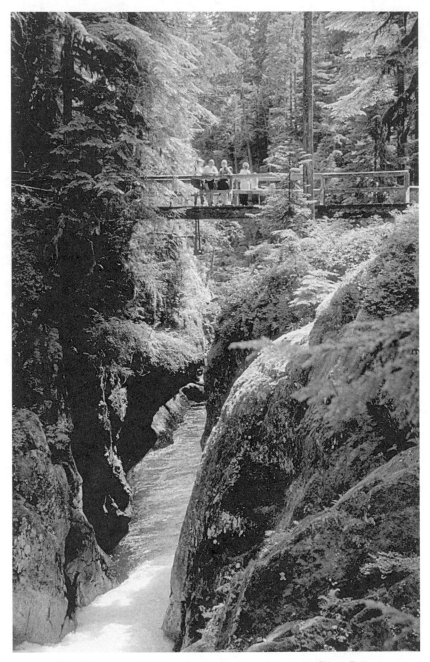

The Ohanapecosh River rips through a gorge near Silver Falls.

26. Three Lakes

RATING	𝍂𝍂𝍂𝍂
DISTANCE	12.0 miles round-trip
HIKING TIME	6.0 hours
ELEVATION GAIN	2,520 feet
HIGH POINT	4,670 feet
DIFFICULTY LEVEL	Difficult
BEST SEASON	September; accessible July to October
PERMITS/CONTACT	Entrance fee; no day-hiking passes required; Ohanapecosh Visitor Center, (360) 569-6046
MAPS	Green Trails No. 271, Bumping Lake; USGS Ohanapecosh Hot Springs
TRAIL NOTES	No dogs or bikes; not a good choice for kids

The Hike

The strain of this climb to three shallow subalpine lakes is lessened greatly by the solitude and the excellent trail, evenly graded and smooth from beginning to end.

Getting There

From the park's Stevens Canyon Entrance on Highway 123, drive 0.2 mile west on Highway 123 to the wide shoulder parking area on the right side of the road. The trailhead, elevation 2,150 feet, is up the road about 100 feet on the opposite side of the highway.

The Trail

The hike to Three Lakes is long and the rewards in terms of grand views are few, but if you are looking for solitude and the chance of seeing or hearing elk in the fall, this is the trail to take. Perhaps because it lacks vistas of Rainier, or possibly because of its length, the Three Lakes Trail sees relatively little use, especially in the autumn. That's too bad, because this is one of the finest trails in the park. The grade is consistent and never too steep, the tread so smooth and free of roots and rocks that you might fall asleep on the way down. It has the feel of one of the old WPA or CCC trails, especially when you can look down to see two or three switchbacks ahead.

The middle of Three Lakes.

Begin by climbing around a forested knoll above Laughingwater Creek, and then drop briefly on one of those switchbacks to pass a swampy lakelet on the left, 1.5 miles from the trailhead. You'll pass the tiny lake and climb again along a wide, rounded ridge beside the creek, switching back several more times past falls and traversing into forested flats beside the creek. In the autumn, Laughingwater is your only water source, and this is the spot to refresh your supply if you have a filter bottle or pump.

The trail leaves the stream and climbs more steeply, switching back up a steep gravelly side hill 3.4 miles from the trailhead. You'll climb steadily from this point, and in about a mile enter subalpine forest. Trees thin and the trail passes along the fringe of a meadow at about 5.2 miles. Just beyond, you'll round a ridge and begin a descent around a wide gully where elk are likely to be seen or heard in the fall.

The trail rounds a second, sharp ridge and drops steeply past the north shore of the first of the Three Lakes. It rounds the lake to the west, and then climbs gently to the Three Lakes Patrol Cabin between the first and second lakes. The third lake lies about 100 yards to the southeast.

Going Farther

Whoa! Those who have the strength to explore after climbing 6 miles will find a fourth lake just west of the first two and—what's this?—a tiny fifth lake about 200 yards east of the third lake. Let's change the name.

CHINOOK PASS

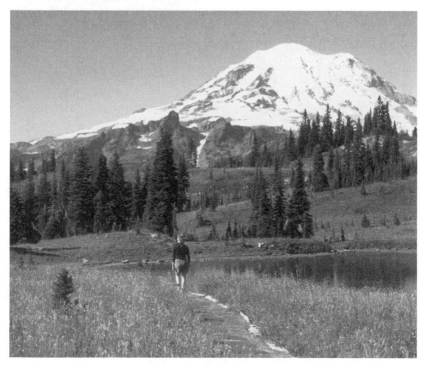

Descending toward one of the picturesque tarns on Naches Peak Loop on a perfect autumn day.

27. Eastside Trail

RATING	
DISTANCE	7.25 miles one way, Deer Creek Trailhead to Stevens Canyon Road
HIKING TIME	3.0 to 4.0 hours
ELEVATION LOSS:	1,032 feet
HIGH POINT	3,232 feet
DIFFICULTY LEVEL	Moderate
BEST SEASON	August to September; accessible June through November
PERMITS/CONTACT	Entrance fee; no day-hiking passes required; Longmire Wilderness Information Center, (360) 569-4453
MAPS	Green Trails No. 270, Mount Rainier East; USGS Chinook Pass
TRAIL NOTES	No dogs or bikes; kids likely to find it monotonous

The Hike

Take an uncrowded, heavily forested, all-downstream river walk parallel to Highway 123 through one of Mount Rainier National Park's most scenic river valleys.

Getting There

The upper trailhead at 3,230 feet is on Highway 123, about 5 miles south of Cayuse Pass and 6 miles north of the park's Stevens Canyon Entrance. Look for the small, unmarked turnout a half mile south of Highway 123's Deer Creek crossing. The lower trailhead at 2,200 feet is the Grove of the Patriarchs parking area, just inside the Stevens Canyon Entrance (see Hikes 24 and 25).

The Trail

Note: The Eastside Trail was damaged in torrential floods in 2006. At press time, numerous bridges and footlogs—notably at Chinook Creek and Deer Creek—had not yet been replaced. Check with the park before you visit.

This is one of our favorite walks for early or late season at Rainier and one of the most pleasant river walks in the park— a great choice anytime, but especially when higher-altitude trails are shrouded in fog and that indefatigable, car-wash rain. The Eastside Trail—little used by Rainier standards—is usually hikeable by early June, and remains so until the snow flies and the roads to the trailhead close. It's a consistently cool, pleasant, private walk through heavy forest in the Chinook Creek and Ohanapecosh River drainages. Arrange to be dropped off at the upper trailhead, and it's a painless downhill walk that most people can do in half a day.

From the upper trailhead, drop quickly 0.4 mile to Deer Creek Camp, turn left (south) and have at it. Don't expect to see the river all the way down; it's out of sight for much of the way, but never far off. Don't worry: It's worth waiting for those moments when the trail reconnects you to the water. Several waterfalls are visible along the route, and highlights include beautiful, whitewater-stream crossings on footlogs at 1.5 miles (Chinook Creek) and 3.0 miles (Ohanapecosh River). You'll wish you'd brought your camera.

The route follows the Ohanapecosh drainage the rest of the way down from the latter crossing. At about 6.4 miles south of Deer Creek Camp, you'll rejoin Rainier's teeming tourist masses at the junction with the Grove of the Patriarchs Trail. If you haven't already done so, walk across the bridge and take the loop (Hike 24). From here, it's only a half mile to the parking lot and—keep your fingers crossed—your waiting car or ride.

Going Farther

Add 3 *very steep* (hence our suggested start) miles to the north end of the one-way trip by beginning at the large, unmarked parking area along Highway 123 just south of Cayuse Pass. Or begin all the way up at Chinook Pass and add 1.3 miles more. Tack on an additional 2.25 miles to the south end by continuing down the Eastside Trail to the Silver Falls Trail and, ultimately, Ohanapecosh Campground (see Hike 25).

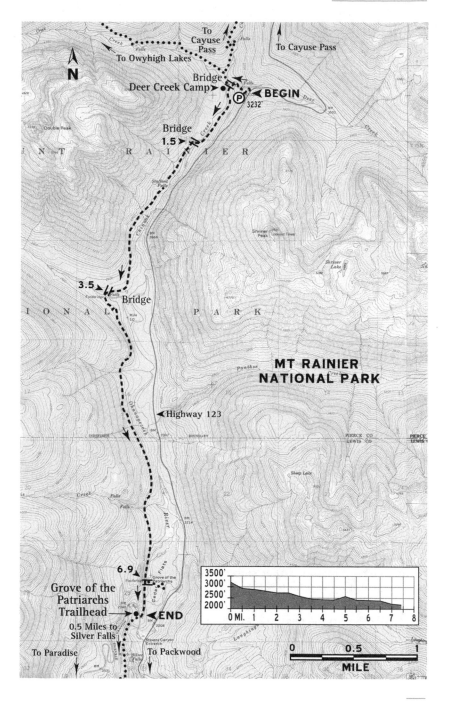

28. Naches Peak Loop

RATING	🚶🚶🚶🚶🚶
DISTANCE	4.5-mile loop
HIKING TIME	2.0 to 3.0 hours
ELEVATION GAIN	700 feet
HIGH POINT	5,900 feet
DIFFICULTY LEVEL	Easy
BEST SEASON	Late July to mid-August; accessible July through October
PERMITS/CONTACT	USFS Northwest Forest Pass required; Snoqualmie Ranger District, Enumclaw Service Center, (360) 825-6585 or Longmire Wilderness Information Center, (360) 569-4453
MAPS	Green Trails No. 270, Chinook Pass and No. 271, Bumping Lake; USGS Chinook Pass, Cougar Lake, White River Park, and Norse Peak
TRAIL NOTES	Kid-friendly; no bikes; dogs okay for only half(!) the hike

The Hike

Embark on a glorious, scenic journey atop the Cascade Crest, with great wildflowers, fall colors, and sweeping vistas of the east side of Mount Rainier.

Getting There

From Enumclaw, follow Highway 410 about 50 miles to Chinook Pass, elevation 5,400 feet. Parking for this hike is available at Tipsoo Lake Picnic Area, and along the highway between the picnic area and the pass, but it's preferable to proceed east of the pass to the parking lots on either side of the highway. The Pacific Crest Trail (PCT) lot on the left side is the largest and most convenient. From there, hike the PCT about a quarter mile south to the loop's starting point: the pedestrian highway overpass at the summit.

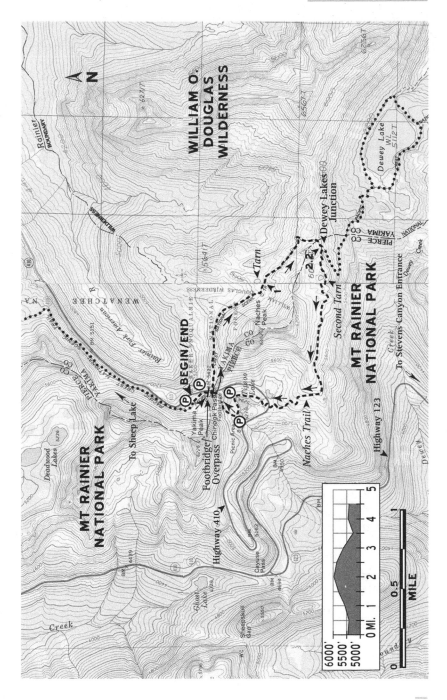

The Trail

On a clear summer or crisp autumn day, this might be the finest day hike in Washington. Plenty of hands shoot up with competitors, but it's hard to argue this hike's attractions: a smooth, even grade, thanks to tens of thousands of pounding feet and the loving care of trail crews. A very gradual grade, especially if you hike the loop in a clockwise direction. A beautiful alpine valley studded with mirror-like tarns, acres of wildflowers, and, in the fall, wild blueberries and stupendous crimson red bushes. And oh, yeah, there's that big mountain over there, shining in all her glory to the west for about half the hike.

Take our word for it and hike the loop clockwise, which just seems to be the *right* way to do this hike. In the first mile, the Pacific Crest Trail rises gently, traversing a slope above a lush valley, where wildflowers will be peeking up at you from mid-July to mid-August. At about 1.0 mile, you'll note a fine, glassy little tarn to the left. The trail climbs slowly and steadily from here through a rocky alpine bowl, with spacious eastern views, beautiful enough to make you forget you haven't seen Rainier yet. Keep your eyes peeled for elk. Eventually the trail climbs several gentle switchbacks to a ridge top southeast of 6,452-foot Naches Peak. Here, about 2.2 miles in, you'll enter the national park and leave the PCT, which drops down to Dewey Lakes, skips across a bunch more mountains, and eventually dumps you out in Mexico.

Back here closer to home, continue straight on what now is the Naches Trail, which leads you to fine views of Mount Adams and the Goat Rocks, to the south. Before long, Rainier comes into view, framed by a series of splendorous, rolling alpine meadows that are adorned with wildflowers in summer and crimson shrubbery in the fall. Passing another small tarn, you'll begin to drop rapidly back toward the highway. Cross the road at about 4.0 miles and find the nature trail around Tipsoo Lake, which ultimately leads back up through the draw to the overpass and parking area.

A word to the wise about dogs: You'll see lots of them on the first portion of this trail, because it's the PCT and, well, dogs are allowed on the PCT, as are horses, llamas, sheep, domesticated wolverines, U.S. senators, and other four-legged creatures. However, at the trail junction 2.2 miles into the hike, you will re-enter the national park, where dogs are expressly forbidden on trails. Your choices at this point are as follows: 1) Go back the way you came and completely miss the best part of the hike; 2) send your dog back on his own, instructing him to open a cold one and fire up the air conditioner in the Blazer; 3) hide the dog in your day pack, beneath the Power Bars; 4) build a fire and cook and eat your dog, thus ensuring you'll have the strength to continue; or 5) wantonly and openly defy the law, risking Lord-knows-what kind of retribution. No pressure or anything, but it's all up to you.

Going Farther

At the park border, you can follow the PCT almost 700 vertical feet down to Dewey Lakes, adding about 2.25 miles to the loop hike (5 miles if you hike all the way around the larger lake).

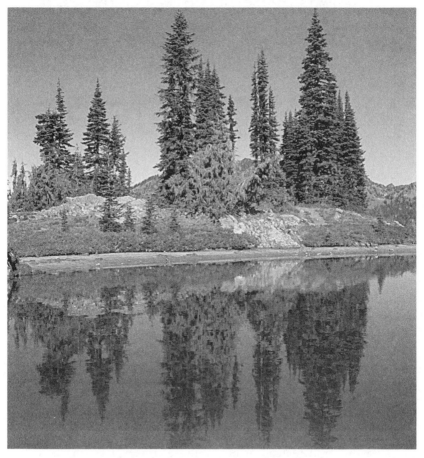

A small tarn about a mile along the Naches Peak Loop.

29. Sheep Lake

RATING	𝍏 𝍏 𝍏
DISTANCE	3.8 miles round-trip
HIKING TIME	2.0 hours
ELEVATION GAIN	1,350 feet
HIGH POINT	5,730 feet
DIFFICULTY LEVEL	Moderately difficult
BEST SEASON	August; accessible July to October
PERMITS/CONTACT	USFS Northwest Forest Pass required; Snoqualmie Ranger District, Enumclaw Service Center, (360) 825-6585
MAPS	Green Trails No. 271, Bumping Lake and No. 270, Mount Rainier East; USGS Chinook Pass
TRAIL NOTES	Leashed dogs okay; kid-friendly

The Hike

The possibility of sunshine on this family hike east of the Cascade Crest makes the climb to a clear alpine lake more inviting. By climbing steeply another mile on the Pacific Crest Trail, you'll gain a great view of Rainier from 6,300-foot Sourdough Gap.

Getting There

From Enumclaw, follow Highway 410 about 50 miles over Chinook Pass to the second big parking area on the left side of the road, just outside the Mount Rainier National Park boundary. The trailhead, elevation 5,400 feet, is located at the horse loading ramp at the east end of the parking area.

The Trail

Here's a place where you can see and feel the difference that only a few hundred yards can make in the climate. The minute you cross Chinook Pass to the east, you'll see a change in the kinds of trees and wildflowers decorating the slopes—especially along the southeast-facing slope you'll traverse for the first mile of this hike.

Begin by following the horse trail as it climbs and switches back to join the Pacific Crest Trail (PCT), 100 yards from the trailhead. Using this trail instead of beginning at the PCT trailhead will enable you to stay upwind of what has got to be one of the stinkiest outhouses on the face of the planet. On a buggy summer's day, however, a quick stop in the outhouse is a sure guarantee for keeping all right-thinking pests at bay for at least twelve hours.

The trail traverses the steep side hill above Highway 410 for more than a mile, making this part of the walk a bit noisier than most backcountry trails. At 1.2 miles, the trail turns to climb into a quiet alpine glade and leaves the noise of the highway behind. You'll cross a meadow underneath a steep ridge and climb steeply for about 120 vertical feet to Sheep Lake, 1.9 miles from the trailhead. This is a good picnic spot and turnaround point for families with younger children.

Going Farther

The PCT passes Sheep Lake and becomes a steep, rocky climb for 1 mile and several switchbacks to Sourdough Gap. At 6,370 feet, the gap is 600 feet above the lake. You'll see a way trail just beyond the gap leading to a rocky low saddle to the north. Walk to the saddle on this trail for a good view of Rainier and look down onto Upper Crystal Lake (Hike 31). It is a short but steep climb down

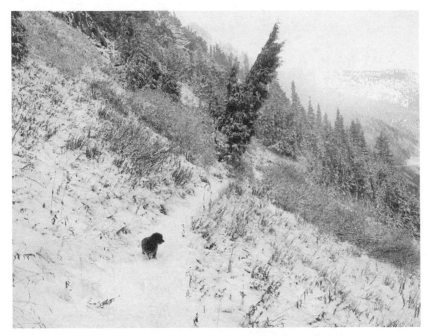

Autumn snowfall covers the trail to Sheep Lake.

to the lake, where you could link with the Crystal Lakes Trail for a one-way or key-exchange hike—assuming you could convince someone to make the longer, steeper climb from the Crystal Lakes trailhead.

WHITE RIVER/SUNRISE

Tall trees fill most Rainier river valleys.

30. Noble Knob

RATING	🚶🚶🚶🚶
DISTANCE	7.0 miles round-trip
HIKING TIME	3.5 hours
ELEVATION GAIN	800 feet
HIGH POINT	6,011 feet
DIFFICULTY LEVEL	Moderately difficult
BEST SEASON	August; accessible July to October
PERMITS/CONTACT	USFS Northwest Forest Pass required; Snoqualmie Ranger District, Enumclaw Service Center, (360) 825-6585
MAPS	Green Trails No. 239, Lester; USGS Noble Knob
TRAIL NOTES	Leashed dogs okay; bikes allowed; kid-friendly

The Hike

Walk along a sunny ridge blanketed by purple lupine to a splendid view of the east side of Rainier and the icy stretch of Emmons Glacier.

Getting There

From Greenwater, drive 13.3 miles south on Highway 410 to Forest Road 7174, on the left. Turn left on FR 7174 and follow it to Corral Pass, about 6.5 miles on a steep, lumpy dirt road. Take the left fork of the road at Corral Pass for the Noble Knob trailhead or, for more parking, continue to the right 0.2 mile to the large parking area at the Corral Pass Campground. The Noble Knob trailhead is 5,650 feet above sea level.

The Trail

Save this hike for a late summer day when you can see forever, because you can definitely see forever along this trail. Okay, maybe "forever" is a slight exaggeration. But with the number of close-up views, "forever" will seem irrelevant.

Look west to Rainier and the Emmons Glacier, where you can see with the naked eye climbing routes etched into the ice, and with binoculars, watch climbers negotiating the massive crevasse at the

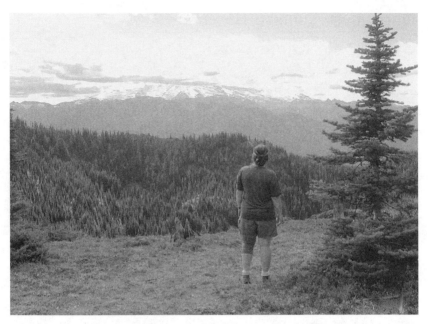

Clouds hide the top of Rainier from Noble Knob.

top of the route. If you've already been there and done that, take the hike to Noble Knob on a day when you can't see any of that stuff. Wildflowers are more showy in the diffuse light provided by fog and you won't be troubled by squadrons of horseflies.

Either way, find the trail at the north end of the parking lot, or, if you are in the mood for an immediate climb to the broad ridge above, begin by following the old road to the east. Both trails join a half mile north, but the trail that climbs east gains and loses several hundred feet and is longer by a half mile, while the northerly trail simply traverses the mountainside. The first half mile of the northerly trail traverses through shady alpine forest before striking the junction with the upper trail at **0.6** mile. Keep left and walk into open hillside created by an old forest fire now overgrown with bear grass, lupine, and other alpine wildflowers.

At **1.8** miles, you'll arrive at the junction with the Deep Creek Trail. Stay right and hike along the ridge, drop to a wide, flat saddle, climb a steep hillside, and round a ridge to traverse open hillside and alpine evergreen groves to a rocky peak directly south of Noble Knob.

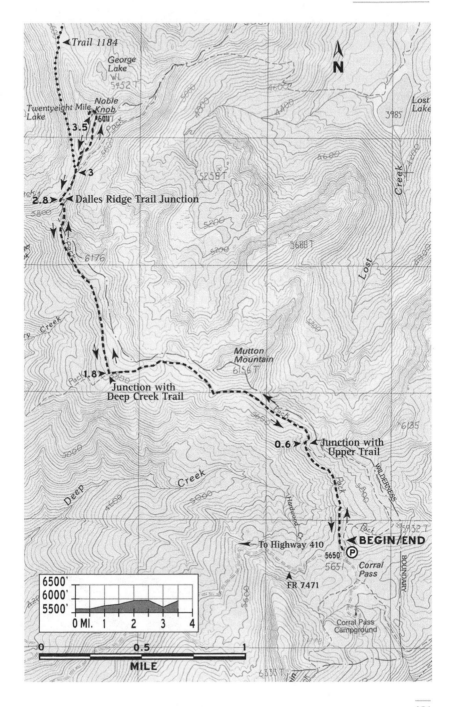

Trail 1184

George
Lake
WL
5952 T

Noble
Knob
6011'

Twentyeight Mile
Lake

3.5

3

2.8 Dalles Ridge Trail Junction

6176

1.8 Junction with
Deep Creek Trail

Mutton
Mountain
6156 T

0.6 Junction with
Upper Trail

Lost
Lake
3985

5258 T

5688 T

6185

Deep Creek

To Highway 410

BEGIN/END

5650'
5651

Corral
Pass

FR 7471

Corral Pass
Campground

6500'
6000'
5500'

0 MI. 1 2 3 4

0   0.5   1
MILE

The trail rounds the peak and drops steeply to a switchback and junction with the Dalles Ridge Trail at **2.8** miles. Keep right and drop to the flat saddle below Noble Knob, directly to the north. You'll find a junction with two trails at the flat saddle, **3.0** miles from the trailhead. Stay right at the first fork and, in 10 feet, left at the second fork. The way to Noble Knob briefly climbs the west shoulder before switching back and, in a climbing traverse, circling the peak to the east to arrive at the summit in 0.5 mile.

Just below the rocky summit is a wide, flat campsite for picnics with a great mountain view, complete with a 10-foot rock scramble to a Noble-looking Knob.

Going Farther

Lake George, directly below Noble Knob to the north, is the closest of several spots to cool off on a hot day. Follow the trail back to the three-way trail junction and turn right on Trail 1184, which traverses under the west side of Noble Knob. At about 0.6 mile from the trail junction, look for a way trail leading right in 0.2 mile to the lake.

Noble Knob provides a noble perch for a noble view.

31. Crystal Lakes

RATING	🚶🚶🚶🚶
DISTANCE	6.0 miles round-trip
HIKING TIME	3.5 hours
ELEVATION GAIN	2,300 feet
HIGH POINT	5,825 feet
DIFFICULTY LEVEL	Moderately difficult
BEST SEASON	August to September; accessible July to October
PERMITS/CONTACT	Entrance fee; no day-hiking passes required; Sunrise Visitor Center, (360) 663-2425
MAPS	Green Trails No. 270, Mount Rainier East; USGS White River
TRAIL NOTES	No dogs or bikes; okay for kids

The Hike

This is an increasingly steep trail to two alpine lakes whose clarity may have something to do with their name.

Getting There

From the junction of Highway 410 and Crystal Mountain Boulevard, follow Highway 410 south for 4.6 miles to the trailhead, elevation 3,500 feet, just across the road from the former site of a Washington Department of Transportation equipment shed.

The Trail

The hike to Crystal Lakes is a popular one, especially in the summer. But those who wait until fall will be rewarded with fewer crowds and—promise not to tell anyone—some of the finest huckleberries in the known universe.

It was at Crystal Lakes, back in 1982, that strange, purple, cloven footprints were found on the trail leading down from the upper lake. Because no purple track led up to the lake, it was first believed by some Naches Tavern regulars in nearby Greenwater that aliens had landed at the lakes. Later the tracks were found to be those of a bull elk which had wandered through the huckleberry patch west of the lake and left berry-juice hoofprints for a half mile down the trail. Feel free to check our research on this point.

The trail begins climbing immediately in switchbacks through thick forest. It's only moderately steep at this point and on parts of the pathway you can actually catch your breath before the next hill. At 1.3 miles, you'll find the Crystal Peak Trail junction. Stay left, here—unless you'd like to climb 1.7 miles to a lookout with a stunning view of Rainier. That's something you'll not get at the lakes.

Hikers headed for the lakes begin a steeper climb past the junction, emerging from the forest onto an avalanche slope about 1.5 miles from the trailhead. The route crosses the path of the slide several times as it switches back to the lakes. Near the top of the avalanche path, you'll get a great view of Mount Rainier and the White River valley to the west. The Mountain ducks behind Crystal Peak at this point.

At 2.3 miles, you'll strike a trail that leads down to the lower and smaller Crystal Lake. This might be the best goal for day-hikers with small children—but if they've got any hiking left in those small feet, encourage them to march on to the higher lake. Though there are no more switchbacks, the trail steepens and begins a long, ascending traverse up the western slopes of Crystal Mountain. Hikers may spot mountain goats in the rocks above the trail, and elk frequent this area in the fall.

The climb ends at **3.0** miles as the trail rounds the east side of the lake. To find the huckleberries that remain after the great alien invasion of '82, head for the gentle slopes on the west side of the lake. Those of you who have Polartec-lined innards may enjoy a swim in these icy waters.

Going Farther

Though no maintained trail exists, a way trail leads from the upper lake at Crystal Lakes southeast toward Sourdough Gap and the Pacific Crest Trail (PCT). It's possible to turn the Crystal Lakes Trail into a one-way hike by connecting to the PCT via the ridge above Sheep Lake (see Hike 29). You can then hike out to Chinook Pass.

In summer, other hikers often make a one-way trek of the Crystal Lakes hike by either climbing the cat track or road—or by riding the chairlift—to the summit of Crystal Mountain Ski Area. From there they descend to the lakes and out to the highway.

Sitka valerian, a common sight in Rainier meadows.

32. Owyhigh Lakes

RATING	🥾🥾🥾🥾
DISTANCE	7.0 miles round-trip
HIKING TIME	3.5 hours
ELEVATION GAIN	1,300 feet
HIGH POINT	5,100 feet
DIFFICULTY LEVEL	Moderate
BEST SEASON	July to September; accessible July to October
PERMITS/CONTACT	Entrance fee; no day-hiking passes required; Sunrise Visitor Center, (360) 663-2425
MAPS	Green Trails No. 270, Mount Rainier East; USGS Mount Rainier East
TRAIL NOTES	Kid-friendly

The Hike

Enjoy a moderate climb to quiet alpine meadows dotted by shallow lakes that reflect the crags of the Cowlitz Chimneys and Governors Ridge. Hikers with two cars have an 8.8-mile, one-way option.

Getting There

From the park's White River Entrance on Highway 410, drive 2.1 miles to the parking lot on the right side of the road. The trailhead, elevation 3,750 feet, is across the road.

The Trail

The hike to Owyhigh Lakes is not recommended for neurotics, simply because you'll go nuts trying to figure out the best time for this walk. If you go in the summer, you'll have the opportunity to wade through mounds of wildflowers. If you go in the fall, you'll miss most of the wildflowers, but have a far greater opportunity of sharing the lake view with herds of elk. Perhaps the best advice is this: If you have trouble deciding, save your neuroses for more important matters. Do the hike once in summer and once in the fall. Maybe because this hike offers no views of that big mound of whipped cream that draws most people to Rainier, this trail often

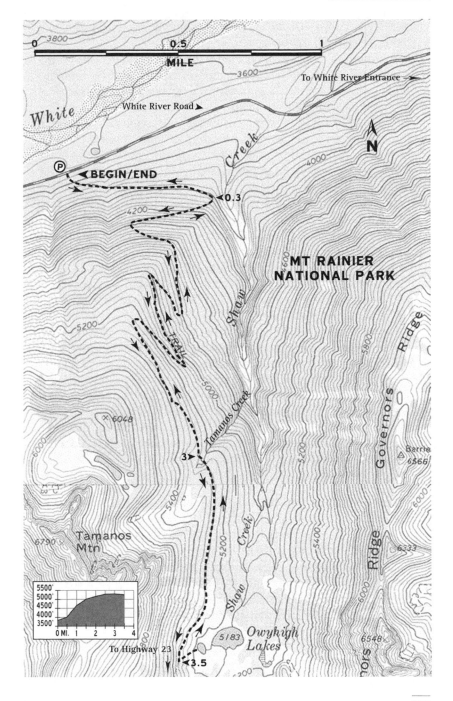

sees fewer crowds. On an autumn weekday, there's a chance you'll have the lakes all to yourselves.

Begin by walking a short 0.1 mile through forest before starting a series of long switchbacks up the broad shoulder of Tamanos Mountain. The trail is wide and it may seem less steep because of its even grade and smooth tread.

You'll strike the first of six switchbacks at about 0.3 mile, with a view down to the polished boulders of Shaw Creek. The trail continues to climb through deep forest up the ridge, which affords hikers peek-a-boo views of the road climbing to Sunrise across the White River valley.

The climb through the woods is steady, though never steep enough to discourage young hikers. At 3.0 miles, you'll cross a footlog at Tamanos Creek, where a green meadow marked by a way trail stretches steeply up. Cross the footlog back into forest to a junction with the side trail leading down to Tamanos Creek Camp. Stay to the right here, and follow the trail as it levels off and contours the final 0.5 mile into alpine meadowland above Owyhigh Lakes.

The lakes are about 100 feet below the trail on the left, and those visiting the shoreline and meadows around the lakes often leave the trail at first sight of the lakes. No sign marks the lakes and no maintained trail drops into the broad plain around them; hikers who stay on the main trail to the south end of the tarns will find a way trail leading along the inlet stream down to water's edge.

Now, neurotics who have ignored our advice and chosen to go on this hike in the summer can slap and scratch at their black-fly bites. Maybe next time, you'll wait until the fall.

Going Farther

Hikers with autos parked at the Owyhigh Lakes trailhead and at the Deer Creek trailhead off Highway 123 (see Hike 27) can make a one-way hike by meeting at the 5,400-foot pass about 0.5 mile south of the lakes. This is the high point of the hike and a good place to exchange car keys. From there, one-way hikers would continue 3 miles through alpine meadows and forest, switching back down and descending another 2 miles to Boundary and Deer Creek, and then climbing in steep switchbacks 0.4 mile and 300 feet to the Deer Creek trailhead.

33. Summerland

RATING 🚶🚶🚶🚶🚶
DISTANCE 8.4 miles round-trip
HIKING TIME 5.0 hours
ELEVATION GAIN 2,140 feet
HIGH POINT 5,950 feet
DIFFICULTY LEVEL Moderate
BEST SEASON Late July to September; accessible July to October
PERMITS/CONTACT Entrance fee; no day-hiking passes required; Sunrise Visitor Center, (360) 663-2425
MAPS Green Trails No. 270, Mount Rainier East; USGS White River Park, Chinook Pass, Mount Rainier East, Sunrise
TRAIL NOTES No dogs or bikes; great way to wear out kids 10 and up

The Hike

A memorable—and often very crowded—stroll takes you through several miles of forest lands along Fryingpan Creek, and then steeply up for a final mile to picturesque Summerland Camp, one of the park's most famous subalpine destinations.

Getting There

From the park's White River Entrance on Highway 410, proceed just under 3 miles to the Wonderland Trail's Fryingpan Creek trailhead, elevation 3,810 feet. Parking is on either side of the road; the trail begins on the left (southwest) side, near the bridge. Parking is at a premium here on summer weekends, and rangers frown on parking along the shoulderless highway—arrive early.

The Trail

We'll lay out the only drawback right up front: crowds. Don't expect any subalpine solitude here. Summerland, one of the park's most popular day-hike destinations, draws hundreds of hikers on summer weekends. But you'll see why. The walk, almost all on the famed Wonderland Trail, begins gently in cool forest along

Fryingpan Creek, with a few sneak peeks of jagged peaks on the far side, but mostly you're surrounded by emerald forest. At about 1.5 miles, the grade steepens a bit. Keep cruising up to about 2.0 miles, where you'll cross a clearing filled with asters and other wildflowers, in season.

At about 3.0 miles, the trail opens up to its one major stream crossing, on footlogs, over Fryingpan Creek. It's a great rest spot; some hikers turn around here, content with the forest walk. If you're going on, break out that do-rag and dunk it in the icy creek: The trail gets steep from here on out, gaining about 800 feet, most of that in the last mile. You'll climb steadily through the trees to a southward bend in the trail, then continue up brushy, steep switchbacks dotted by avalanche lilies in July and August. This portion of the trail can stay snow covered until late July; use caution.

At 4.2 miles, the trail levels out in flat-out gorgeous meadows and subalpine forest near Summerland, a backcountry camp where the five designated sites are tucked into a grove of trees near the stone shelter. All are usually booked solid throughout the summer. Well, duh—aside from the outhouse, everything here looks grand: abundant wildflowers and wild animals, and postcard views of Rainier, the Fryingpan Glacier, Little Tahoma, and Goat Island Mountain. Take a load off your feet, soak up some sun, and memorize the moment. On a favorable summer day, it doesn't get much better. The trip out is quick and pleasant, assuming you're not fighting a big blister and/or nasty packs of blackflies.

Going Farther

The trail continues another 2 miles and about 850 vertical feet up the rocky moraine of the Fryingpan Glacier to Panhandle Gap, elevation 6,800 feet—worth the trip if you have the time. For a spectacular, one-way shuttle hike, descend south from Panhandle Gap on the Wonderland Trail to Indian Bar Camp. Continue down Cowlitz Divide to Box Canyon (16.6 total miles; see Hike 23) or southeast via the Olallie Creek Trail to the Stevens Canyon Entrance or Highway 123 near Ohanapecosh Campground (about 18 total miles).

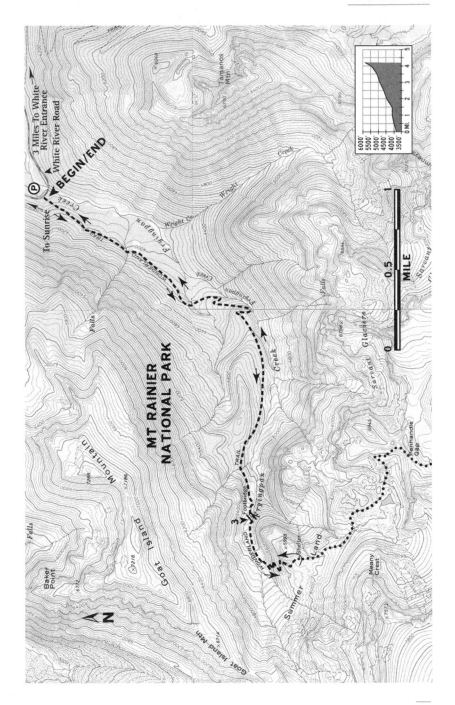

34. Emmons Moraine/Glacier Basin

RATING 🚶🚶🚶🚶

DISTANCE 4.0 miles round-trip to end of Emmons Moraine/6.2 miles round-trip to Glacier Basin

HIKING TIME 2.0 hours/4.0 hours

ELEVATION GAIN 850 feet/1,650 feet

HIGH POINT 5,200 feet/6,000 feet

DIFFICULTY LEVEL Easy/Moderate

BEST SEASON July to September; accessible early July to October

PERMITS/CONTACT Entrance fee; no day-hiking passes required; Sunrise Visitor Center, (360) 663-2425

MAPS Green Trails No. 270, Mount Rainier East; USGS Sunrise

TRAIL NOTES No dogs or bikes; Emmons Moraine is great for kids

The Hike

Hike a river valley to dueling payoffs: a high vista over the massive Emmons Glacier and a great alpine basin in a park area once home to mining activity.

Getting There

From the park's White River Entrance on Highway 410, proceed just under 4 miles to the White River Campground turnoff. Turn left and continue 1.5 miles, through the campground, to the hiker and climber day-use parking area on the left (north) side of the road. Walk east on the campground road through Loop D to the Glacier Basin trailhead, elevation 4,350 feet.

The Trail

Note: This trail was badly damaged by the floods of 2006. At press time, the Emmons Moraine Spur Trail was inaccessible, and the Glacier Basic Trail had been temporarily rerouted pending a trail reconstruction in 2009 or 2010.

This isn't just a great hike; it's a great *combination* of hikes, allowing you to design a daylong outing to suit the time available,

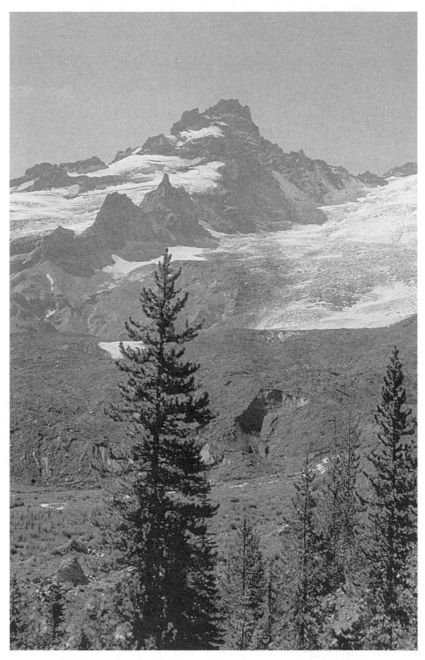

The Emmons Glacier creeps along beneath Little Tahoma.

or just your mood. From White River Campground, the path ascends gently on an old road grade along the Inter Fork of the White River. Believe it or not, mining equipment made its way through here from the 1890s through the 1950s, thankfully with little success.

About 1.0 mile up the way, the Emmons Moraine Trail crosses the creek and exits to the left (south). Hike up the loose sand on the moraine as far as you like. After about only about a quarter mile up the trail, you can climb atop the moraine for a killer view of the ground-out path of the massive Emmons Glacier—the largest by volume in the Lower 48 states—and on up the valley to the foot of the glacier itself. Look closely: This icy behemoth, although a shadow of its former self, is actually bigger than it looks. Rocky debris from a gigantic rockslide off Little Tahoma Peak covered the middle of the glacier almost twenty years ago; the slide is only now making its way down toward the glacier's toe. The maintained trail ends in half a mile at 5,200 feet, but there's no need to go all the way to the end for the view.

To reach Glacier Basin, return to the main trail and keep ascending gradually until about 2.5 miles, where there is some old mining junk along the trail. From here, the grade steepens for the rest of the way to Glacier Basin Camp at 3.1 miles, where wildflowers burst forth in season. Most of Rainier is blocked from view, but there's plenty to see. Watch for mountain goats on the slopes of Mount Ruth and The Wedge, at the head of the basin.

Going Farther

A number of way trails sprout out from the basin, including a steep path down to the Inter Fork and a climbers' trail up to 9,400-foot Camp Schurman, tucked behind Steamboat Prow at the junction of the Winthrop and Emmons Glaciers. Schurman is the departure point for Rainier summit expeditions up the Emmons Glacier. At this writing, most of those hikes were guided commercially by International Mountain Guides, the company owned by noted Himalayan mountaineer Eric Simonson, of recent Mallory and Irvine Research Expedition fame.

You can reach Glacier Basin on an all-downhill, one-way route by beginning at Sunrise. Hike the Sunrise Rim and Burroughs Loop Trails (Hike 37) east to the Burroughs Mountain Trail, plunge downhill on steep switchbacks to Glacier Basin (6.3 miles), and exit east at White River Campground (9.5 miles).

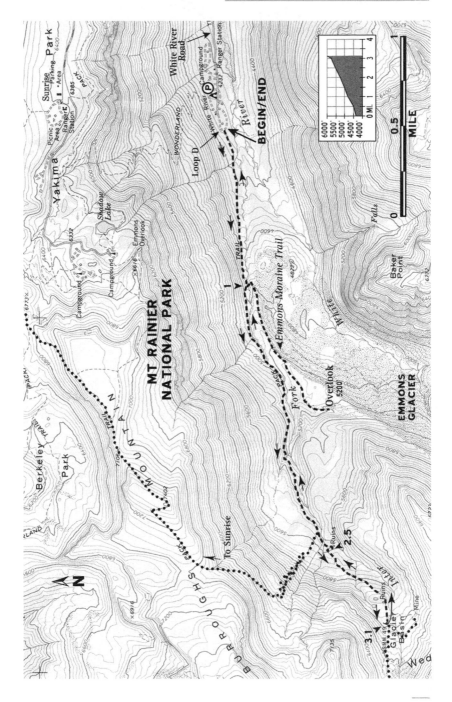

35. Palisades Lakes

RATING	🚶🚶🚶
DISTANCE	7.5 miles round-trip
HIKING TIME	3.0 to 4.0 hours
ELEVATION GAIN	1,600 feet
HIGH POINT	6,150 feet
DIFFICULTY LEVEL	Moderately difficult
BEST SEASON	Mid-July to mid-August; accessible July to October.
PERMITS/CONTACT	Entrance fee; no day-hiking passes required; Sunrise Visitor Center, (360) 663-2425
MAPS	Green Trails No. 270, Mount Rainier East; USGS Sunrise and White River Park
TRAIL NOTES	No dogs or bikes; a not-so-great choice for kids

The Hike

Descend sharply to find a string of a half-dozen scenic alpine lakes in this protected valley. The Palisades Lakes Trail is a good foul-weather alternative to more exposed hikes at Sunrise, though the lakes can be *very* buggy in midsummer.

Getting There

From the park's White River Entrance on Highway 410, proceed 11 miles on White River Road to the well-marked Sunrise Point parking area, on a hairpin curve at 6,150 feet. The trail begins across the road, near the crux of the hairpin curve.

The Trail

The Palisades Lakes Trail is an oddity because it starts high and drops like a rock, plummeting more than 500 feet in the first mile. After a series of sharp switchbacks, you'll enter a valley dotted by a half-dozen fine alpine lakes. The first, Sunrise Lake, is dead ahead at the bottom of the hill. But nicer ones await: Take the main path to the right and enter a pleasant, fairly flat stretch of alternating meadows and forest. Clover Lake, the largest in this

A meadow near Clover Lake, largest of the Palisades Lakes.

cluster and a true beauty, complete with a sandy beach, comes up on your right in about 1.5 miles. It's a great picnic spot. And check out the five-way echo that results if you let out a war whoop from the small knoll along the shoreline.

The trail from here climbs a ridgeline, and then drops steeply over the other side to more meadows and a junction, at 2.5 miles. A short spur trail leads up to Hidden Lake, a gorgeous, glacial-cirque lake below Sourdough Mountain. On the opposite side of the main trail, look for Dick Lake Camp and another spur leading to Tom, Dick, and Harry Lakes.

Continue a mostly flat mile north on the main trail, through some great open meadows, to a trail junction. The left fork leads to Upper Palisades Lake and its backcountry campsites. Continue right to see Lower Palisades Lake from near the end of the main-tained trail.

Upper Palisades Lake, elevation 5,840 feet, is definite Fujichrome material. It's set below the Palisades, a fascinating formation of striated rock. Wildflowers are glorious here in season. Watch for elk and deer throughout this valley, and remember: Save some gas for the trip out, where you'll climb 900 feet in elevation on the way back to the trailhead. Be prepared for a short but very steep climb up the ridge back to Clover Lake, followed by that blasted last half mile of pure vertical back to the car! Something about saving it for the end makes it twice as ominous.

36. Silver Forest/Emmons Vista

RATING	
DISTANCE	2.0 miles round-trip
HIKING TIME	45 minutes
ELEVATION GAIN	170 feet
HIGH POINT	6,400 feet
DIFFICULTY LEVEL	Easy
BEST SEASON	Mid-July to mid-August; accessible July to October
PERMITS/CONTACT	Entrance fee; no day-hiking passes required; Sunrise Visitor Center, (360) 663-2425
MAPS	Green Trails No. 270, Mount Rainier East; USGS Sunrise and White River Park
TRAIL NOTES	No dogs or bikes; easiest Sunrise view hike for kids and seniors

The Hike

This easy, mostly level stroll leaves the Sunrise complex, ambles to a grand vista of the Emmons Glacier and Mount Rainier, and continues beyond through a pleasant forest of silver firs with more great mountain views.

Getting There

From the park's White River Entrance on Highway 410, proceed 14 miles to Sunrise, elevation 6,400 feet. The trail begins on the south border of the parking area straight across from the Sunrise Ranger Station; follow signs to Emmons Vista.

The Trail

If you're a hiker who wants the best views with the least amount of sweat and blisters, this one's for you. The Silver Forest Trail is an easy walk, slightly downhill at first, about 0.3 mile to Emmons Vista, an impressive stone viewing platform with a billion-dollar view of Rainier. Interpretive signs describe the forces behind (and under and all around) the massive Emmons Glacier. On a clear day in midsummer, you can see the ant trail of climbers ascending to the 14,411-foot summit.

Don't stop here, though. The Silver Forest Trail continues east, following the ridgeline, through meadows which, in midsummer, are ablaze with an impressionist painter's palette of orange and magenta paintbrush, blue alpine lupine, lavender alpine asters, yellow daisies, and other magnificent wildflowers. In fall, low huckleberry bushes turn crimson. Rainier is omnipresent to the south. Take your time, breathe in that sweet, thin alpine air, watch for butterflies, and be sure to carry plenty of film. Most of this trail's (small) elevation gain is on the way out.

Note: If you're looking for the best pictures of Rainier from here, skip that extra latte and get here in the morning; the sun is directly over The Mountain by midafternoon in summer. Also note that no water is available along the trail.

Going Farther

This hike can be combined with the Sunrise Rim Loop (Hike 37) for a hike of about 5 miles.

A classic Rainier sight: Emmons Vista on a clear day.

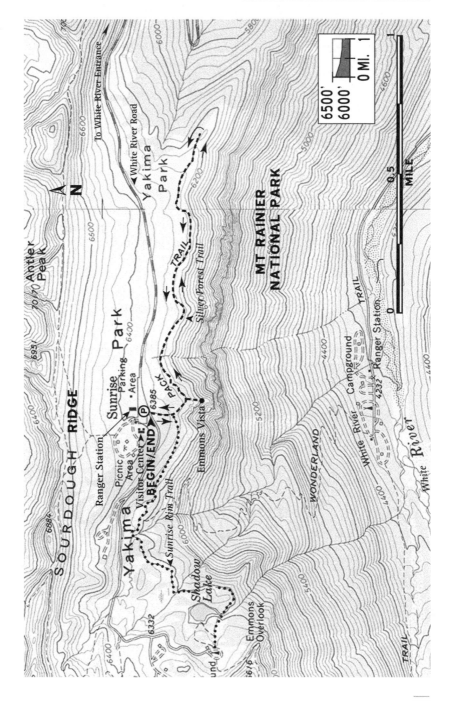

37. Sunrise Rim Loop

RATING	🥾🥾🥾🥾
DISTANCE	3-mile loop
HIKING TIME	1.5 hours
ELEVATION GAIN	250 feet
HIGH POINT	6,400 feet
DIFFICULTY LEVEL	Easy
BEST SEASON	Mid-July through mid-September; accessible July to October
PERMITS/CONTACT	Entrance fee; no day-hiking passes required; Sunrise Visitor Center, (360) 663-2425
MAPS	Green Trails No. 270, Mount Rainier East; USGS Sunrise
TRAIL NOTES	No dogs or bikes; great family hike

The Hike

Follow an easy, family-friendly loop that showcases gorgeous wildflower meadows, mountain views, and plentiful wildlife—all within 1.5 miles of Sunrise Visitor Center.

The stunning alpine scenery of Yakima Park.

Getting There

From the park's White River Entrance on Highway 410, proceed 14 miles to Sunrise, elevation 6,400 feet. The trail begins on the south border of the parking area across from the Sunrise Ranger Station; follow signs to Sunrise Camp.

The Trail

Here's your Whitman's Sampler of the Sunrise area: a lightly used route (by Sunrise standards, at least) combining a trail to Sunrise Camp and a park service access road with fine alpine views of its own. From the parking lot, begin at the same south-side trailhead used to access the Silver Forest Trail (Hike 36). At the first junction, stay right on the Sunrise Rim Trail. For the next mile, you'll drop gently through open meadows dotted by the stately subalpine firs common in this area, all the while enjoying stupendous views of Rainier and the green forests and meadows of Yakima Park.

At about 0.5 mile, you'll meet a junction with the Wonderland Trail, which drops sharply 2.6 miles to White River Campground. Stay straight on what now is technically the Wonderland Trail, toward Sunrise Camp.

At about 1.0 mile, you'll pass glassy, shallow—and yes, shadowy—Shadow Lake. About a half mile farther is Sunrise Camp, elevation 6,260 feet. In days of yore, this was a car camp, now it's a backcountry site available by reservation (file it away as a good first-time backpacking destination for kids).

For your return, follow the same route you came, or try something new: Walk the (closed) gravel service road departing north from the campground. It's lightly traveled, pleasantly graded, and views are wide open from either side. Keep your eyes peeled for Rocky Mountain elk around the road's first bend. It's an easy walk from here back to Sunrise, although most of the hike's modest elevation gain comes on the way out.

Note: Carry plenty of water—it's scarce along the route.

Going Farther

From the rear of Sunrise Camp, a trail climbs sharply to the top of Burroughs Mountain (Hike 41). You can walk the first 0.25 mile or so to an impressive overlook of the Emmons Glacier.

If the weather looks good and your knees feel better, continue on the Burroughs Loop Trail and then the Burroughs Mountain Trail 1.3 miles—and nearly 1,000 vertical feet—up to the First

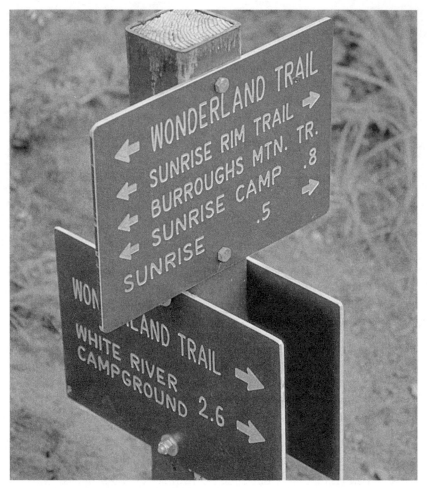

Hikers can walk the Wonderland Trail downhill from Sunrise to White River Campground.

Burroughs summit at 7,300 feet. Note that this may involve a hazardous snowfield crossing before late summer. Follow the Burroughs Loop Trail northeast back to a junction with the Sourdough Ridge Trail at Frozen Lake, and turn right to return to Sunrise. It makes a spectacular loop of about 5.2 miles.

Or, back near Sunrise Camp, follow the Wonderland Trail up to Frozen Lake and walk back to Sunrise via the Sourdough Ridge Trail, making a loop of about 4 miles.

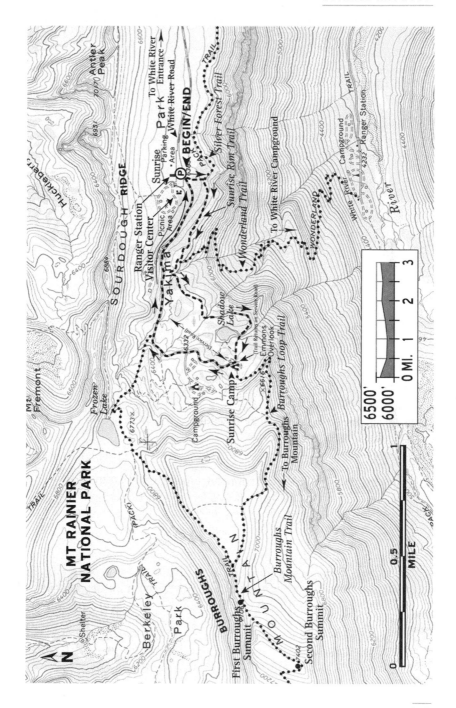

38. Sourdough Ridge/Dege Peak

RATING	🚶🚶🚶
DISTANCE	4.0 miles round-trip
HIKING TIME	1.5 hours
ELEVATION GAIN	600 feet
HIGH POINT	7,006 feet
DIFFICULTY LEVEL	Easy
BEST SEASON	Mid-July to mid-August; accessible July to October
PERMITS/CONTACT	Entrance fee; no day-hiking passes required; Sunrise Visitor Center, (360) 663-2425
MAPS	Green Trails No. 270, Mount Rainier East; USGS Sunrise and White River Park
TRAIL NOTES	No dogs or bikes; kid-friendly

The Hike

Take the whole family on this hike and enjoy sweeping views south to Little Tahoma, the Emmons Glacier, and the northeast face of Mount Rainier, and north along the Cascade chain as far as Mount Baker. Be sure to carry plenty of water and screen up—the entire route is exposed to sun.

Getting There

From the park's White River Entrance on Highway 410, proceed 14 miles to Sunrise, elevation 6,400 feet. Begin to the right of the restrooms and walk to the trail's start at the picnic area. On the early portion of the route, follow signs to Dege Peak.

The Trail

On a sunny summer day, the only better place to see the Cascades stretching from Rainier to the north may well be from the summit of The Mountain itself. The Sourdough Ridge Trail, which technically runs east–west above Sunrise all the way from Sunrise Point to Frozen Lake (see also Hikes 39 and 40), is a major thoroughfare in the Sunrise area, carrying thousands of hikers to higher-level trailheads, mostly northwest of Sunrise. But the crowds are

The Sourdough Ridge Trail runs right along the tree line above Sunrise.

thinner, and views even grander, if you ascend the broad, graveled entry path from Sunrise and turn right (east) on the Sourdough Ridge Trail and follow the ridgeline toward Dege Peak.

Remember: The ridge top is 6,800 feet, so if you're unaccustomed to exercise at high altitude, you'll be feeling the big squeeze on your lungs. But this is a pleasant, mostly flat walk once the ridge is gained at 0.3 mile. The views are spectacular in both directions, and wildflowers will be magnificent on the south-facing slopes in midsummer.

At 1.8 miles, a short spur leads up to the top of Dege Peak, elevation 7,006. It's a supreme vista. Look for Rainier, of course, but also the Sarvent Glaciers below the Cowlitz Chimneys, due south; the White River drainage and Highway 410, to the east; Sunrise and Clover Lakes of the Palisades chain (see Hike 35) directly below to the northeast; and the Stuart Range, Glacier Peak, and Mount Baker far off to the north. If it's very clear, you can even see the Olympic Mountains from here.

Going Farther

If you can arrange for a ride, keep descending down the ridge for another steep mile to the Sunrise Point parking lot, for a one-way hike of about 3 miles.

39. Huckleberry Creek/Forest Lake

RATING	
DISTANCE	5.0 miles round-trip
HIKING TIME	2.5 hours
ELEVATION GAIN	500 feet in, 1,300 feet out
HIGH POINT	6,900 feet
DIFFICULTY LEVEL	Moderate
BEST SEASON	Mid-July to September; accessible mid-July to October
PERMITS/CONTACT	Entrance fee; no day-hiking passes required; Sunrise Visitor Center, (360) 663-2425
MAPS	Green Trails No. 270, Mount Rainier East; USGS Sunrise
TRAIL NOTES	No dogs or bikes; okay for kids

The Hike

Climb up and over Sourdough Ridge to a pleasant mountain lake. You'll get fewer great Rainier views—but also fewer people—than on other Sunrise-area trails.

Descending Sourdough Ridge near the Huckleberry Creek Trail junction.

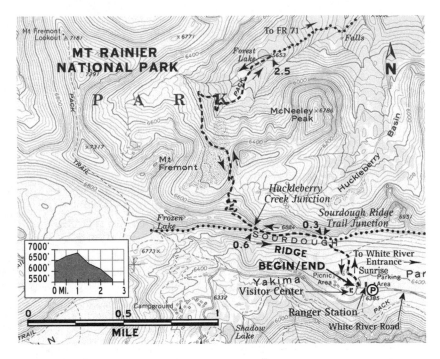

Getting There

From the park's White River Entrance on Highway 410, drive 14 miles to Sunrise, elevation 6,400 feet. Begin to the right of the restrooms and walk to the trail's start at the picnic area. Follow signs to the left (west) toward Frozen Lake, and then Huckleberry Creek Trail.

The Trail

The first portion of this hike follows the same route as many other trails in this section: up to the top of Sourdough Ridge, and then a short distance west to a junction with the Huckleberry Creek Trail at **0.6** mile. Follow the Huckleberry Creek Trail right and moments later you'll begin dropping steadily, almost 1,300 feet in a shy **2.0** miles, through a fascinating variety of terrain. The upper portion is rocky and inhospitable (beware of snow lingering here into August most years); the central portion wanders through scenic, subalpine parkland dotted with red heather; the lower area, near Forest Lake, is deciduous forest.

The central portion between 7,317-foot Mount Fremont (left/west) and 6,786-foot McNeeley Peak (right/east), is the most scenic.

Keep your eyes peeled for mountain goats on the back side of Fremont. In season, meadows around Forest Lake are ripe with wildflowers. Have a hearty lunch and head back up the trail. The view of Rainier as you come over the rise of Sourdough Ridge is unforgettable.

Going Farther

The Huckleberry Creek Trail leads a total of 8.3 miles from Sourdough Ridge to a low trailhead (3,000 feet) on Forest Road 73, in Mount Baker–Snoqualmie National Forest. It's a popular one-way, downhill day hike or backpack route (Forest Lake has one backcountry campsite).

Subalpine firs on the return from Forest Lake.

40. Frozen Lake/Mount Fremont Lookout

RATING	🚶🚶🚶🚶
DISTANCE	5.4 miles round-trip
HIKING TIME	3.0 hours
ELEVATION GAIN	781 feet
HIGH POINT	7,181 feet
DIFFICULTY LEVEL	Moderate
BEST SEASON	Mid-July through mid-September; accessible July to October
PERMITS/CONTACT	Entrance fee; no day-hiking passes required; Sunrise Visitor Center, (360) 663-2425
MAPS	Green Trails No. 270, Mount Rainier East; USGS Sunrise
TRAIL NOTES	No dogs or bikes; good for older kids

The Hike

Enjoy a memorable walk along Sourdough Ridge to a five-way trail junction near Frozen Lake, and beyond to a mountain lookout tower where mountain goats and other wildlife often linger.

Getting There

From the park's White River Entrance, proceed 14 miles to Sunrise, elevation 6,400 feet. Begin to the right of the restrooms and walk to the trail's start at the picnic area. Follow signs to the left (west) toward Frozen Lake.

The Trail

There's really no place like this in the Cascades, the West, the country, or maybe the world. The walk to Frozen Lake and Mount Fremont is a rite of passage for Northwestern tykes. Many people's first shaky steps off the pavement and onto the moon-rock dust of Rainier's stunning alpine tundra happen along this route. And the fact that it's just the first step to many great leaps gives this hike a special appeal.

The first part of this walk follows the path taken to many other popular hikes in this area: up to Sourdough Ridge, then left (west) on the Sourdough Ridge Trail, with grand views of Rainier to the south and the entire Cascade chain to the north. At one point,

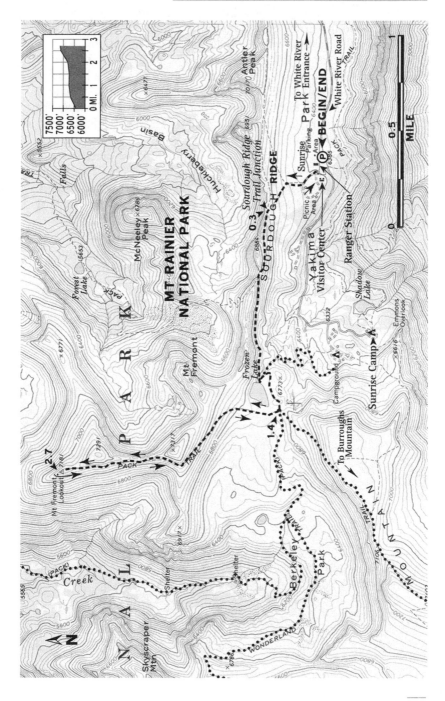

you'll stand in a draw on a ridge top no wider than a street, and have trouble deciding which way to focus your attention.

The path drops slightly, crossing a rocky slope (nice trail work, that retaining wall!), and then climbs gently to a hard left-hand turn at Frozen Lake. The lake, a pretty, deep-aqua pool, is fenced off, because it's the drinking water supply for Sunrise. Take the left turn and follow the path around and up to a major trail junction at 1.4 miles. Major as in, sort of mind boggling. No fewer than five trails converge at this point; it's the Rainier alpine hiker freeway interchange. Plop yourself down on a rock here and drink in the views of Rainier (lower flanks), Burroughs Mountain, Yakima Park and Sunrise, and Mount Fremont. You can also take in the vast plains of the Wonderland Trail leading toward Berkeley Park.

You can make this your turnaround point without feeling completely cheated, but far greater splendors await. Follow signs to the Mount Fremont Trail, which skirts Frozen Lake to the north, climbing steadily up the ridge in a long, 1.3-mile straight line with no switchbacks. Don't forget to check your rearview mirror for Rainier—preferably not while you're along the steep drop-off near the top of the trail, on the shoulder of Mount Fremont. The path descends slightly to the lookout at **2.7** miles and **7,181** feet. The view is stunning, from Rainier all the way to the North Cascades.

The long, steady rise to Mount Fremont Lookout.

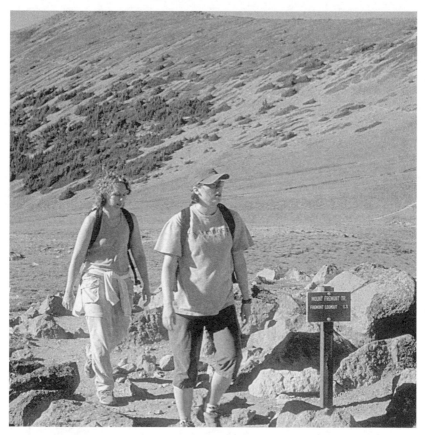

Hikers at the five-way trail junction near Frozen Lake.

(Be glad you weren't here in the winter of 2006 when a violent storm blew the roof completely off the lookout!) Watch for mountain goats grazing on the slopes nearby, and whatever you do, don't contribute to the further Power Bar addiction of local marmots.

Note: Carry plenty of water—it's scarce along the route.

Going Farther

Burroughs Mountain (Hike 41), Berkeley Park (Hike 42), Sunrise Camp (via the Wonderland Trail), and other destinations all are accessible from the trail super-junction at Frozen Lake.

41. Burroughs Mountain

RATING	🚶🚶🚶🚶🚶
DISTANCE	6.2 miles round-trip via Frozen Lake; 6.7-mile loop via Sunrise Camp
HIKING TIME	3.0 to 4.0 hours
ELEVATION GAIN	1,000 feet
HIGH POINT	7,400 feet
DIFFICULTY LEVEL	Moderately difficult
BEST SEASON	Mid-August to mid-September; accessible late July to late October, with some potentially hazardous snow crossings until mid-August or later
PERMITS/CONTACT	Entrance fee; no day-hiking passes required; Sunrise Visitor Center, (360) 663-2425
MAPS	Green Trails No. 270, Mount Rainier East; USGS Sunrise
TRAIL NOTES	No dogs or bikes; not a great choice for kids, especially when snow is present

The Hike

One of the most spectacular alpine day hikes from Sunrise, the Burroughs Mountain Trail is a fairly strenuous climb along the top of Burroughs Mountain in a bizarre, tundra-like environment with incredible views throughout.

Getting There

From the park's White River Entrance on Highway 410, proceed 14 miles to Sunrise, elevation 6,400 feet. Begin to the right of the restrooms and walk to the trail's start at the picnic area. Follow signs to the left (west) toward Frozen Lake.

The Trail

Like many other city-sized chunks of rock around here, Burroughs is a fascinating geologic oddity. It's actually part of an old lava flow, left exposed after softer earth was eroded away on either side. As such, and given its high altitude, the upper mountain supports only tiny vegetation growth; stay on the trail, for your own

The terrain on the Burroughs Mountain Loop is rocky, barren, and stunning.

safety and that of the plants, which take years to grow back after you trample them.

Burroughs can be approached from either of two ways: via the Sourdough Ridge and Frozen Lake route described here, or by hiking the Sunrise Rim Trail toward Sunrise Camp (Hike 37) and approaching Burroughs's ridgeline from the southeast via the Burroughs Loop Trail. To add variety to your hike, consider going up in one direction and coming down the other: Making this quasi loop adds only about 0.5 mile to the overall distance.

We prefer the Frozen Lake approach, however, primarily for its dramatic, in-your-face view of Rainier's summit as you climb the Burroughs Mountain ridgeline. To get there, walk the Sourdough Ridge Trail from Sunrise up the ridge and to the left, toward Frozen Lake (see Hike 40). At the five-way trail junction near Frozen

Lake (1.4 miles, 6,785 feet), stay left where signs point up the hill, southwest, to Burroughs Mountain.

The trail ascends a steady mile. Views dead ahead are of Rainier's summit—particularly beautiful as it falls under ghostly shadows in late afternoon. Below to the north is the great, flat, green (or bronze, in early fall) plateau of the Berkeley Park area—a shocking contrast to the sheer, rocky vertical terrain you're crossing. Watch for marmots on the uphill slopes here. One major safety caveat: This stretch of trail crosses a steep, extremely hazardous snowfield that often lingers well into August, and in some years never fully melts out. Do not attempt to cross it without lug-soled boots and an ice ax or other means to self-arrest. A tiny slip here can be—and has been—deadly.

The trail finally flattens out at the top of First Burroughs at 2.4 miles and about 7,100 feet. Just short of the summit is a junction with the Burroughs Loop Trail, descending to the Sunrise Rim Trail. Stay straight, drop a short way, and then climb again 0.75 mile to Second Burroughs summit, elevation 7,402 feet. On a clear day, grander alpine vistas are tough to find anywhere on Planet Earth. As you face Rainier, the summit, Little Tahoma Peak, and the massive Emmons (left) and Winthrop (right) Glaciers all look close enough to touch. Tiny wildflowers and blooming sprigs of heather are found here in late summer.

Going Farther

The path drops from here another 1.4 miles—and a toe-blackening 1,900 feet—to Glacier Basin and an exit at White River Campground (Hike 34). Save that for another lifetime. Turn around and retrace your steps through the moonscape back to First Burroughs and a right-hand (east) turn down the Burroughs Loop Trail. It's about 3.0 miles back to Sunrise this way via Sunrise Camp, Shadow Lake, and the Sunrise Rim Trail (see Hike 37). If you go this way, note that another steep snowfield, which also usually lingers into late summer, must be crossed about 0.5 mile above Sunrise Camp. Use extreme caution.

Note: Carry plenty of water—it's scarce along the route.

42. Berkeley Park

RATING	🥾🥾🥾
DISTANCE	7.8 miles round-trip
HIKING TIME	4.0 hours
ELEVATION GAIN	1,600 feet
HIGH POINT	6,773 feet
DIFFICULTY LEVEL	Moderate
BEST SEASON	August; accessible July to October
PERMITS/CONTACT	Entrance fee; no day-hiking passes required; Sunrise Visitor Center, (360) 663-2425
MAPS	Green Trails No. 270, Mount Rainier East; USGS Sunrise
TRAIL NOTES	Kid-friendly; no dogs or bikes

The Hike

The walk to Berkeley Park takes you first up, and then down through alpine tundra to a wide meadow filled with just about every wildflower to be found around Mount Rainier.

Getting There

From the park's White River Entrance on Highway 410, proceed 14 miles to Sunrise, elevation 6,400 feet. The trailhead begins on the north side of the parking lot at the paved access to the Sourdough Ridge Trail.

The Trail

Sunrise gets mighty crowded in the late summer, but the meadows of Berkeley Park might not be visited as frequently simply because day-hikers have so many trails from which to choose. Since the walk to Berkeley involves one steady, 800-foot climb—and a total ascent of 1,200 feet—on the way home, fewer hikers might choose it as their destination.

Regardless, there's plenty of views and wildflower watching to share with everyone you encounter. Begin by climbing from the trailhead to a junction with the Sourdough Ridge Trail, **0.1** mile from the parking area. Keep left at the junction and climb briefly to a junction with the Huckleberry Creek Trail. Stay left here and

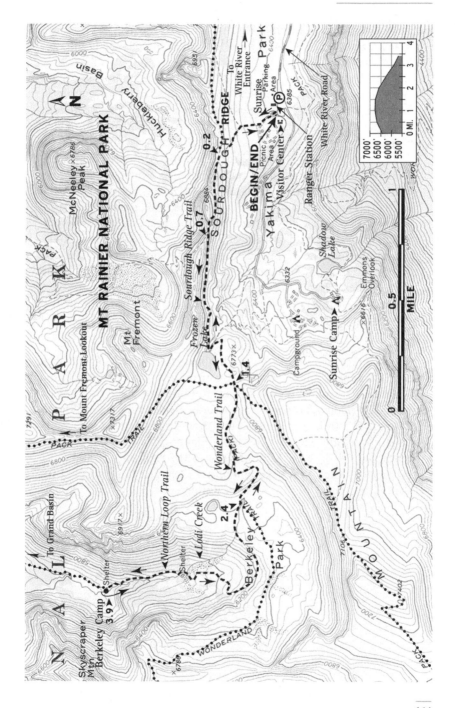

continue along Sourdough Ridge to the five-way trail junction near Frozen Lake, 1.4 miles from the trailhead, and the high point for this hike.

Hey: Flip a coin. Do you think a guidebook should give you every answer? Okay, follow the Wonderland Trail as it goes west from the junction beyond Frozen Lake and begins to descend gently under the cliffs of Burroughs Mountain (see Hike 41). Crumbled parts of the mountain decorate the hillside on your left as you descend and pikas cry "knee!" from their rock thrones.

The trail continues to drop into a wide, flat meadow to a junction with the Northern Loop Trail at 2.4 miles. Turn right on the Northern Loop Trail and follow it as it descends more steeply into Berkeley Park, the valley formed by Lodi Creek. Above the flower-filled valley is Mount Fremont, on the right, and Skyscraper Mountain on the left. The trail winds through the valley for about a mile before entering the subalpine forest and coming to Berkeley Camp at 3.9 miles. This is the turnaround point for day-hikers, and a good spot for those who carry filter pumps or bottles to replenish their water supply.

Going Farther

Strong hikers who don't mind climbing 1,500 vertical feet back to the trailhead should consider continuing past Berkeley Camp for another 3 miles to Grand Park, a mile-long meadow flat as a pancake griddle. The return trip affords a splendid view of Mount Rainier. The trail first climbs, and then descends past the camp, leveling off and striking the Lake Eleanor Trail junction at 6.9 miles. Follow the Lake Eleanor Trail to the right into Grand Park. When you reach the place where a 747 might land safely, turn around and check out the view of Rainier.

43. Skyscraper Pass

RATING	🚶🚶🚶
DISTANCE	7.2 miles round-trip
HIKING TIME	3.5 hours
ELEVATION GAIN	1,300 feet
HIGH POINT	6,773 feet
DIFFICULTY LEVEL	Moderate
BEST SEASON	August to September; accessible mid-July to October
PERMITS/CONTACT	Entrance fee; no day-hiking passes required; White River Wilderness Information Center, (360) 663-2273
MAPS	Green Trails No. 270, Mount Rainier East; USGS Sunrise
TRAIL NOTES	Kid-friendly; no dogs or bikes

The Hike

Wander up and down—then up—through flowery meadows to an airy view of The Mountain that you may well enjoy with company of the mountain goat kind.

Getting There

From the park's White River Entrance on Highway 410, proceed 14 miles to Sunrise, elevation 6,400 feet. The trailhead begins on the north side of the parking lot at the paved access to the Sourdough Ridge Trail.

The Trail

The hike to Skyscraper Pass might be another trail many of the hikers at Sunrise avoid, simply because it involves a moderate climb on the return trip. Views from the pass and the chance to picnic with some of the local wildlife might make the hike worth the effort. You'll share the trail with hikers bound for Mount Fremont for the first 1.4 miles and with Berkeley Park–bound hikers for another mile, until you swing off on the Wonderland Trail to the pass, a high saddle underneath Skyscraper Mountain.

The first portion of the trail is on the same route you may (or may not) have already hiked on Hikes 39–42: from the Sunrise

A hiker on the Wonderland Trail, with Rainier's summit in the distance.

parking area, 0.3 mile up the Sourdough Ridge Trail to the ridge top above Sunrise Camp, proceeding west to a five-way junction at Frozen Lake, 1.4 miles. Stay left on the Wonderland Trail, which heads west beyond Frozen Lake and begins a gentle descent under the rocky flank of Burroughs Mountain.

The trail drops through two flat meadowland benches, reaching a junction with the Northern Loop Trail at 2.4 miles. Turn left at this junction, climb over a knoll, and begin a long ascending traverse to Skyscraper Pass, 3.6 miles from the trailhead. The climb to the pass is on a moderate grade, but may seem steeper on a dry, hot day. In the autumn, the upper tributaries to Lodi Creek may be dry, so plan to bring plenty of water with you.

The pass, at 6,700 feet, is at about the same elevation as Frozen Lake. Granite Creek tumbles from the Winthrop Glacier and Sluiskin Mountain guards the valley to the west.

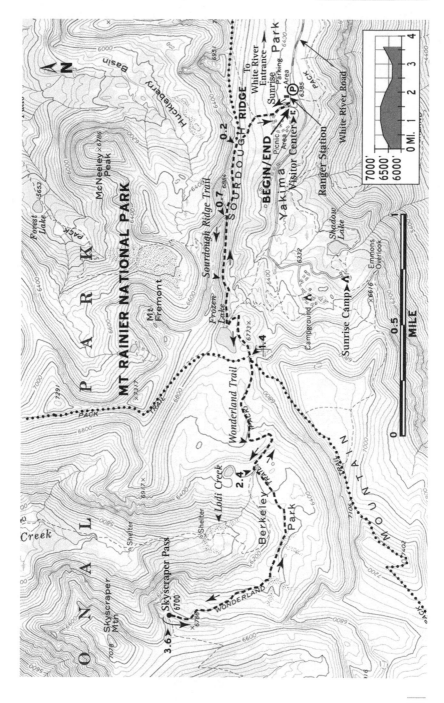

CARBON GLACIER/
MOWICH LAKE

Cataract Creek displays one of the features from which it got its name.

44. Green Lake

RATING	🚶🚶🚶
DISTANCE	6.0-mile round-trip hike/bike to trailhead; 3.6-mile round-trip hike
HIKING TIME	2.0 hours (trail only)
ELEVATION GAIN	1,120 feet
HIGH POINT	3,220 feet
DIFFICULTY LEVEL	Moderate
BEST SEASON	August to September; accessible July to October
PERMITS/CONTACT	Entrance fee; no day-hiking passes required; Carbon River Ranger Station, (360) 829-9639
MAPS	Green Trails No. 269, Mount Rainier West; USGS Carbon River
TRAIL NOTES	Kid-friendly; no dogs or bikes

The Hike

Enjoy a great family hike past spectacular Ranger Falls to a quiet (in the autumn) lake surrounded by an avalanche-swept hillside and forest.

Getting There

From Puyallup, follow Highway 410 about 13 miles east to Buckley. Turn right (south) onto Highway 165, crossing the bridge over the Carbon River. Bear left to the Mount Rainier National Park Carbon River entrance. Walk or bicycle 3.0 miles up the Carbon River Road to the trailhead on the left.

The Trail

Note: This is one of many day hikes in the Carbon River drainage that have become very long day hikes or bike/hikes because of the closure to automobiles, perhaps permanently, of the washed-out Carbon River Road at the park entrance, 5 miles below Ipsut Creek Campground. (The road's future is uncertain; it is not likely to be reopened to Ipsut Creek, but one option at press time is to reopen the road partway to vehicles. The distance listed above is assuming the road is closed at the Park entrance; call for current

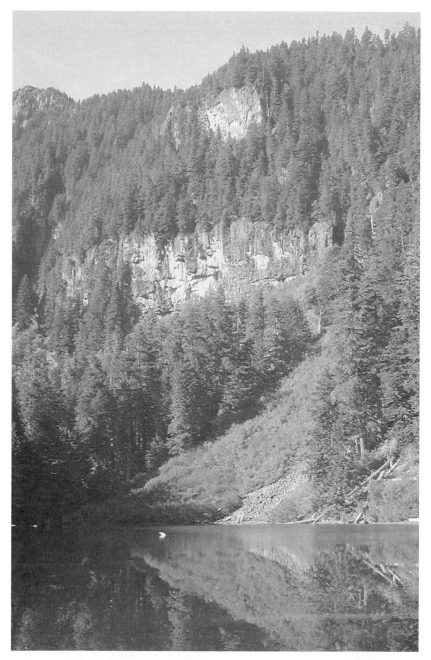

Green Lake makes a good destination for families with children.

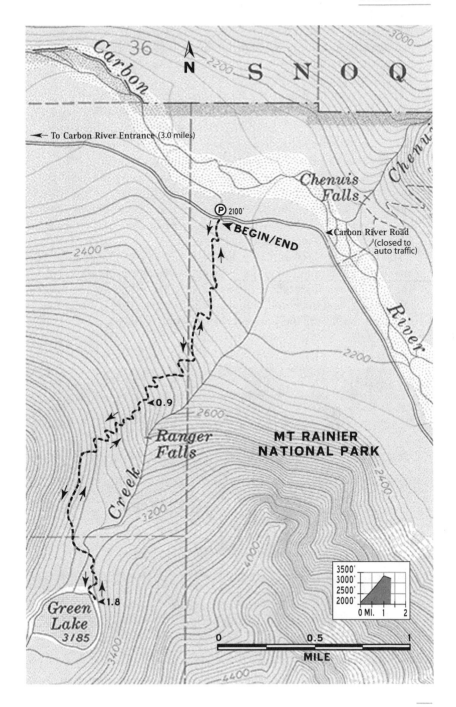

To Carbon River Entrance (3.0 miles)

Carbon

N

S N O Q

Chenuis
Falls

ⓟ 2100'

BEGIN/END

Carbon River Road
(closed to
auto traffic)

River

2400

2200

0.9

2600

Ranger
Falls

MT RAINIER
NATIONAL PARK

2400

Creek

3200

4000

1.8

Green
Lake
3185

3400

3500'
3000'
2500'
2000'
0 MI. 1 2

0 0.5 1
MILE

4400

information.) In the meantime, hikers might look at this as a rare opportunity to ride their mountain bikes into the park and leave them at the trailhead before making a day hike that's likely much less crowded than in previous years.

This is a popular hike in the late spring and summer, often yielding (forgive me) sole-to-soul hiking. So wait until mid-September, when you will share the trail with fewer people and perhaps more elk. For maximum solitude and a better chance at seeing wildlife, plan this walk in the early morning or evening.

The youngsters will flat-out love this hike, not only for the shallow, log-walking lakeshore at the destination, but for the wide number of diversions along the way. A cattle prod might come in handy to keep the kids moving, especially when they spot the three fallen Really Big Trees that bridge the trail.

You'll wander the forest flats beside Ranger Creek for about 0.1 mile before beginning to climb in switchbacks alongside the creek. The trail tunnels underneath the first Really Big Tree, switches back to a second, and eventually climbs to a third tree that is likely too high and too far off the trail to beckon young climbers.

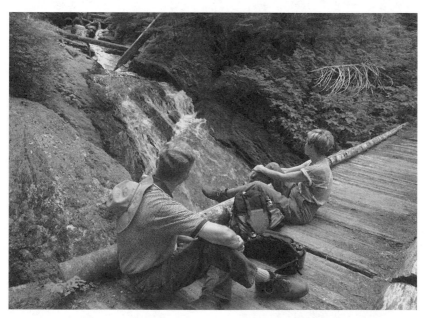

Falls along the Ipsut Creek Trail to the Really Big Tree.

At about **0.7** mile, you'll find a way trail at one switchback leading to low cascading falls that some hikers might mistake for Ranger Falls. Nope; you must continue climbing for another 0.2 mile to another switchback and signed trail leading 100 yards to the left to a fenced overlook of the much higher and more spectacular Ranger Falls.

Back on the trail, you'll continue climbing in switchbacks another quarter mile, and then traverse along the hillside to a footlog crossing of Ranger Creek at **1.5** miles. Cross the creek, which is wide and still, and climb to the high point of the hike, 3,220 feet, before dropping steeply down to Green Lake's north shore.

The maintained trail ends at the lakeshore, **1.8** miles from the trailhead. Log hoppers can follow the shoreline west to the mouth of the outlet and the open shoreline to the southwest.

45. Really Big Tree/Ipsut Pass

RATING	🚶
DISTANCE	10.0 miles round-trip hike/bike to trailhead; 6.4-mile round-trip hike
HIKING TIME	4.0 hours (trail only)
ELEVATION GAIN	2,800 feet
HIGH POINT	5,100 feet
DIFFICULTY LEVEL	Difficult
BEST SEASON	August; accessible July to October
PERMITS/CONTACT	Entrance fee; no day-hiking passes required; Carbon River Ranger Station, (360) 829-9639
MAPS	Green Trails No. 269, Mount Rainier West; USGS Golden Lakes
TRAIL NOTES	Kid-friendly; no dogs or bikes

The Hike

Make a strenuous climb through a forest of really big trees to a conifer said to be the world's largest Alaska Cedar—a real Really Big Tree.

Getting There

From Puyallup, follow Highway 410 about 13 miles east to Buckley. Turn right (south) onto Highway 165, crossing the bridge over the Carbon River. Bear left to the Mount Rainier National Park Carbon River entrance. Walk or bicycle 5.0 miles up the Carbon River Road to the trailhead at the former Ipsut Creek Campground, elevation 2,300 feet.

The Trail

Note: This is one of many day hikes in the Carbon River drainage that have become very long day hikes or bike/hikes because of the closure to automobiles, perhaps permanently, of the washed-out Carbon River Road at the park entrance, 5 miles below Ipsut Creek Campground. (The road's future is uncertain; it is not likely to be reopened to Ipsut Creek, but one option at press time is to reopen the road partway to vehicles. The distance listed above is assuming the road is closed at the Park entrance; call for current information.)

The world's largest Alaska cedar grows right smack dab beside the trail to Ipsut Pass, which could come as something of a surprise to the good people of Olympic National Park, who claim that the world's largest Alaska cedar is on the Big Creek Trail in the Quinault River valley. Superintendents from each park need to duke it out to determine the champion tree. Nonetheless, if you enjoy looking at big trees, this is a hike for you. You'll first pass by a large Douglas fir whose nurse log long ago turned to forest duff, leaving a cave underneath the tree suitable for hobbits and children alike. The warren even has a window and back door. Shortly after passing the really big fir, you'll encounter a huge Western red cedar. Your aching muscles may at this point try to convince you that this is the genuine Really Big Tree. It is not. You must climb farther.

But first things first: Begin the hike by following the Carbon River Trail from the parking lot, passing the side trail to Ipsut Falls in 0.1 mile. Begin a traversing climb that ends at 0.3 mile from the parking lot at a junction with the Ipsut Pass Trail. Turn right here and begin the serious climbing up the ridge above Ipsut Creek on the right. The trail wastes little time gaining elevation, climbing with few switchbacks through an ancient forest which serves up a blueberry feast in early fall.

You'll find the Douglas fir hobbit house about 1.2 miles from the trailhead, a good turnaround point for families with younger children. The trail continues climbing—more steeply now—and passes the huge red cedar at about 1.4 miles. After switching back once, you'll cross a creek on a footlog and climb to a second creek where a footbridge affords a great spot to get a photo of the splendid cascade on your left. This is the kind of waterfall you'd bring home to meet the parents, although doing so would likely cause substantial grousing from the Department of the Interior.

Now the trail climbs along the crest of a low ridge that divides two branches of Ipsut Creek. Huge conifers provide a hallway through the forest. As the low ridge rises steeply in front of you, you'll begin traversing upward along the right side. The forest thins and trees grow smaller as the valley below opens into an alpine meadow, 2.8 miles from the trailhead.

You leave the forest behind at 3.0 miles and the character of the trail turns from smooth dirt to alpine rock immediately. You'll cross a stream and wet meadow and climb steeply to a grove of Alaska cedars, directly ahead. The trail passes between two really big Alaska cedars on the right and three really big Alaska cedars uphill on the left.

It is difficult to tell which of the trees is largest, but one is the Really Big Tree. It appears that the biggest cedar on the right had a top broken off from an avalanche and the tallest cedar is now the middle one on the left. No sign marked the world record tree in the fall of 2001. But it doesn't matter. None are as large as some of the really big conifers you've seen down the trail. If it is sunny, enjoy the shade these trees give. If it is raining, enjoy their shelter. It's time for a picnic before heading back down.

Going Farther

You can continue up the trail another very steep 0.8 mile, switching back under cliffs to Ipsut Pass, where the trail joins the path to Eunice Lake and Tolmie Peak that comes from Mowich Lake. Other than more exercise, though, there's little point in climbing past the Really Big Tree since you can hike to Ipsut Pass by following the much easier Tolmie Peak Trail 1.5 miles from Mowich Lake (see Hike 50).

46. Carbon Glacier Viewpoint

RATING	🚶🚶🚶🚶
DISTANCE	10.0 mile round-trip hike/bike to trailhead; 7.0-mile round-trip hike
HIKING TIME	3.5 hours (trail only)
ELEVATION GAIN	1,200 feet
HIGH POINT	3,400 feet
BEST SEASON	August to September; accessible July to October
DIFFICULTY LEVEL	Moderate
PERMITS/CONTACT	Entrance fee; no day-hiking passes required; Carbon River Ranger Station, (360) 829-9639
MAPS	Green Trails No. 269, Mount Rainier West; USGS Carbon River
TRAIL NOTES	Kid-friendly; no dogs or bikes

The Hike

Once one of the easiest ways in Mount Rainier National Park to get up close and personal with a real, live glacier, the trek to the snout of Carbon Glacier is now long because of road closures. It's still worth the trek for hardier hoofers.

Getting There

From Puyallup, follow Highway 410 about 13 miles east to Buckley. Turn right (south) onto Highway 165, crossing the bridge over the Carbon River. Bear left to the Mount Rainier National Park Carbon River entrance. Walk or bicycle 5.0 miles up the Carbon River Road to the trailhead at the former Ipsut Creek Campground, elevation 2,300 feet.

The Trail

Note: This is one of many day hikes in the Carbon River drainage that have become very long day hikes or bike/hikes because of the closure to automobiles, perhaps permanently, of the washed-out Carbon River Road at the park entrance, 5 miles below Ipsut Creek Campground. (The road's future is uncertain; it is not likely to be reopened to Ipsut Creek, but one option at press time is to reopen the road partway to vehicles. The distance listed above is

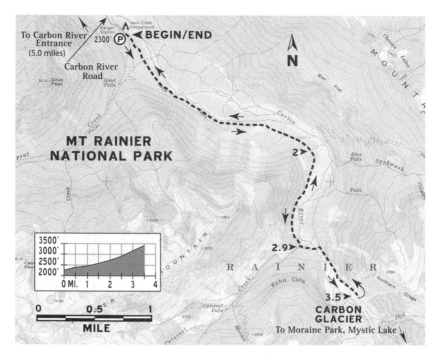

assuming the road is closed at the Park entrance; call for current information.)

The hike to the snout of the Carbon Glacier follows a long-abandoned roadbed and the trail is seldom more than hearing distance away from the silty Carbon River. At the trailhead, the river is fewer than 3 miles from where it gushes from beneath the glacier.

Begin by following the Carbon River Trail in glacier-ground sand through the forest for **0.1** mile to a junction with a side trail to Ipsut Falls. Stay left at the junction and begin a moderate climb through forest that ends **0.2** mile from the trailhead at a junction with the Ipsut Pass Trail. Stay left at this junction as the trail continues to climb more gently through the forest above the river. The trail turns toward the river and rejoins the old roadbed above the watercourse, where the rushing river tumbles boulders clunking downstream.

As the trail rounds a ridge, hikers can get their first view of the glacier, still 1.5 miles upstream. The trail eventually enters the forest and begins to climb away from the main course of the river underneath cliffs and broken shards of the ridge above. At **2.0** miles from the trailhead, you'll find a junction with the Northern

Loop Trail. Stay right and continue to climb gently past Carbon River Camp at **2.8** miles.

Past the camp, the trail drops to a footlog crossing Cataract Creek, just below one of the low falls that gave the creek its name. On the far side of the creek, you'll find a junction with the Seattle Park Trail. Stay left here, and climb a short hill to a suspension bridge over the Carbon River, **3.0** miles from the trailhead. The suspension bridge is a great thrill to cross. It's high above the river and sways and bounces slightly as hikers navigate the planks. You'll see the dirty snout of the glacier upstream from the bridge. In the fall, the tread from the bridge is sometimes removed to avoid damage by heavy winter snows; if the bridge is closed, a well-marked trail leads to footlogs across the river.

Once across the river, turn right on the trail and follow it as it begins to climb steeply under glacier-polished cliffs beside the river of ice. This is the steepest part of the trail, and it reaches a viewpoint of the glacier's frozen leading wave at **3.5** miles from the trailhead.

Pick out a big trailside rock seat and watch the Carbon River being born. A sign warns hikers about straying too close to the ice,

The snout of the Carbon Glacier.

which could crack into chunks definitely too large for your margarita, or spill rocks it carries from above.

Going Farther

Although the glacier viewpoint might be the best turnaround spot for many wilderness pedestrians, the 2,000-foot climb up past Dick Creek Camp to Moraine Park, 6.6 miles from the trailhead, yields splendid views of The Mountain and a spectacular alpine meadow. Strong hikers may choose to continue through Moraine Park to Mystic Lake, a beautiful alpine lake nestled under the north face of Rainier, 7.5 miles from the trailhead.

47. Cataract Camp/Seattle Park

RATING 🧍🧍

DISTANCE 10.0-mile round-trip hike/bike to trailhead; 8.4-mile round-trip hike

HIKING TIME 5.5 hours (trail only)

ELEVATION GAIN 2,400 feet

HIGH POINT 4,700 feet

DIFFICULTY LEVEL Difficult

BEST SEASON July to September; accessible July to October

PERMITS/CONTACT Entrance fee; no day-hiking passes required; Carbon River Ranger Station, (360) 829-9639

MAPS Green Trails No. 269, Mount Rainier West; USGS Golden Lakes

TRAIL NOTES No dogs or bikes; too steep for most kids

The Hike

Climb into an open valley so thick with blueberries you can't return without purple mouth and hands. You'll be surrounded by high cliffs with a wide view of the dark forests of the Carbon River on the way home. Strong hikers can climb another 500 feet and 1.5 miles into beautiful Seattle Park underneath Echo Rock and the Russell Glacier.

Getting There

From Puyallup, follow Highway 410 about 13 miles east to Buckley. Turn right (south) onto Highway 165, crossing the bridge over the Carbon River. Bear left to the Mount Rainier National Park Carbon River entrance. Walk or bicycle 5.0 miles up the Carbon River Road to the trailhead at the former Ipsut Creek Campground, elevation 2,300 feet.

The Trail

Note: This is one of many day hikes in the Carbon River drainage that have become very long day hikes or bike/hikes because of the closure to automobiles, perhaps permanently, of the washed-out Carbon River Road at the park entrance, 5 miles below Ipsut

The trail to Cataract Camp climbs up a valley walled by cliffs.

Creek Campground. (The road's future is uncertain; it is not likely to be reopened to Ipsut Creek, but one option at press time is to reopen the road partway to vehicles. The distance listed above is assuming the road is closed at the Park entrance; call for current information.)

Hikers in search of solitude are likely to find more of it on this trail than on most others around the Carbon River, since it is a long, hard climb past Cataract Camp into the open alpine country of Seattle Park. Begin by following the Carbon River Trail past its junction with a spur trail leading right to Ipsut Falls, at **0.1** mile, and uphill to a junction at **0.3** mile with the Ipsut Pass Trail.

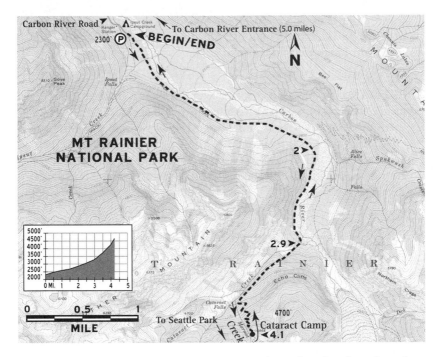

Stay left at this junction and continue along the abandoned road as it alternately winds through forest and beside the silty, raging Carbon River.

At **2.0** miles, you'll strike a junction with the Northern Loop Trail. Stay right at the junction and in another 0.8 mile, pass Carbon River Camp. Drop to a footlog crossing of Cataract Creek where, if you look upstream, you'll get a pretty good idea of how the creek was named. Cross the footlog to find the junction with the trail climbing to Seattle and Spray Parks. Turn right here and begin the serious climbing to Cataract Camp.

The first half mile of this trail climbs in steep switchbacks where the highbush blueberries lining the trail in the fall are likely to slow your pace far more than the grade. The grade lessens somewhat in the next half mile, but the berries do not.

About **3.6** miles from the trailhead, the view up the valley opens to show cliffs of Mother Mountain. The trail switches back and continues to climb above Marmot Creek before arriving at Cataract Camp, **4.2** miles from the trailhead.

The camp makes a good picnic spot and turnaround for most day-hikers. If you've been grazing on berries, perhaps you can save your lunch for another hike.

Going Farther

Hikers looking for more spectacular views and beautiful alpine meadows can continue to climb another 500 feet and 1.5 miles to the lower edge of Seattle Park. From there, the trail continues to climb another 1,200 feet and 1.5 miles to the ridge that divides Seattle Park from Spray Park—but hikers headed there will have a much easier go of it by taking the trail from Mowich Lake (see Hike 51).

48. Yellowstone Cliffs

RATING	
DISTANCE	10.0-mile round-trip hike/bike to trailhead; 10.2-mile round-trip hike
HIKING TIME	6.0 hours (trail only)
ELEVATION GAIN	2,800 feet
HIGH POINT	5,100 feet
DIFFICULTY LEVEL	Difficult
BEST SEASON	September; accessible July to October
PERMITS/CONTACT	Entrance fee; no day-hiking passes required; Carbon River Ranger Station, (360) 829-9639
MAPS	Green Trails No. 269, Mount Rainier West; USGS Carbon River and Sunrise
TRAIL NOTES	No dogs or bikes

The Hike

This is a marvelous workout for wilderness pedestrians in search of an excuse to gobble ibuprofen or to count switchbacks. You'll climb to a good view of some really big rock columns in wide alpine meadows.

Getting There

From Puyallup, follow Highway 410 about 13 miles east to Buckley. Turn right (south) onto Highway 165, crossing the bridge over the Carbon River. Bear left to the Mount Rainier National Park Carbon River entrance. Walk or bicycle 5.0 miles up the Carbon River Road to the trailhead at the former Ipsut Creek Campground, elevation 2,300 feet.

The Trail

Note: This is one of many day hikes in the Carbon River drainage that have become very long day hikes or bike/hikes because of the closure to automobiles, perhaps permanently, of the washed-out Carbon River Road at the park entrance, 5 miles below Ipsut Creek Campground. (The road's future is uncertain; it is not likely to be reopened to Ipsut Creek, but one option at press time is to reopen the road partway to vehicles. The distance listed above is

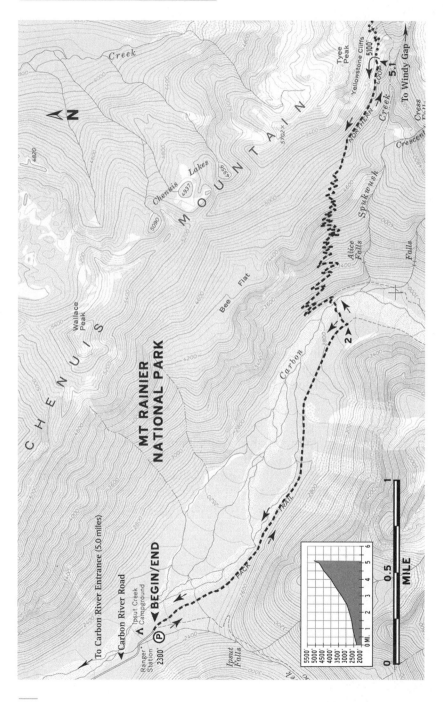

assuming the road is closed at the Park entrance; call for current information.)

Masochistic hikers will be disappointed in the first couple of miles of this trail, because it is relatively easy walking. Sadistic hikers should take their only comfort in this section, knowing the masochists aren't suffering nearly enough.

The trail follows an abandoned road alongside the Carbon River for 2 miles, passing a junction with the Ipsut Falls Trail at 0.1 mile and with the Ipsut Pass Trail at 0.3 mile. Stay left at both these junctions. The trail climbs through forest, under cliffs, and beside the boulder-strewn path of the Carbon River to a junction with the Northern Loop Trail, 2.0 miles from the trailhead. Turn left onto it and descend to the valley floor.

The path winds through the forest and crosses two footlogs to the boulder field shaped by the river. In the fall, the Carbon is usually low and a footlog crossing has been constructed across the pewter ribbons of water. The footlogs, however, are frequently washed out in spring and summer and hikers not wishing to risk fording must continue another mile upstream to the suspension bridge crossing, and then follow the trail downstream on the other side to the Northern Loop Trail.

Once across the footlog, the trail meanders downstream several hundred yards before beginning its steep climb. It gains more than 2,000 vertical feet in the next 3 miles, following thirty-six switch-backs on a steady grade. The path is through the forest, which provides shade and on an autumn day may makes the way seem less steep. The trail never ceases climbing, even when it reaches the junction with the Yellowstone Cliff Camp Trail, 5.1 miles from the trailhead. Here you'll find the first of the alpine meadows, a view of the rock columns of Yellowstone Cliffs, and a good spot beside the trail where—if you are in as good a physical condition as us—you'll flop like an exhausted flounder to the ground, begging for someone to shoot you.

Going Farther

Though it never would cross our minds that any sane hiker would want to continue this painful journey, you can climb another 0.5 mile (and 500 vertical feet) to Windy Gap. It may live up to its name on some days, but on calm autumn afternoons, its meadows make a fine place to wonder why in the world anyone would want to work so hard to get here.

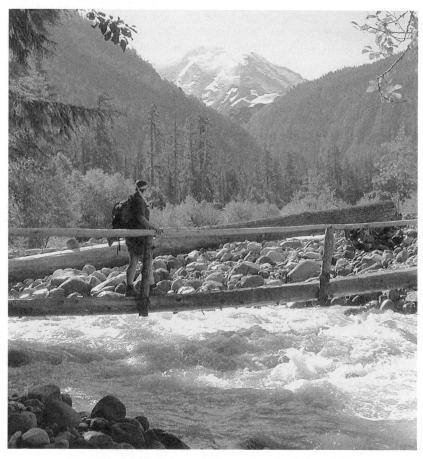

The route to Yellowstone Cliffs crosses the Carbon River
a few miles below the snout of the Carbon Glacier.

49. Mowich River Camp

RATING	🧍🧍🧍🧍
DISTANCE	7.2 miles round-trip
HIKING TIME	4.0 hours
ELEVATION GAIN	2,860 feet
HIGH POINT	4,200 feet
DIFFICULTY LEVEL	Moderately difficult
BEST SEASON	August to September; accessible July to October
PERMITS/CONTACT	Entrance fee; no day-hiking passes required; Carbon River Ranger Station, (360) 829-9639
MAPS	Green Trails No. 269, Mount Rainier West; USGS Golden Lakes
TRAIL NOTES	Kid-friendly; no dogs or bikes

The Hike

This walk is mostly downhill on the way to Mowich River Camp, but the climb back to the trailhead may seem easier because the excellent path is so nicely graded. It's a good hike for a foggy or rainy day.

Getting There

From Wilkeson, follow Highway 165 south for 9 miles to a junction with the Carbon River Road. Continue right (south) on the highway, and proceed about 12 miles to the Paul Peak trailhead on the right (south) side of the road, elevation 3,700 feet. You'll find an unmanned fee station at the parking area, where you can pay the park entrance fee if you don't have an annual pass.

The Trail

Although the peek-a-boo shots through the forest of the North Mowich Glacier are impressive, this hike is mostly short on views. For that reason alone, you might choose a less than perfect day for this walk.

But here are a couple of other good reasons for adding this trek to your list of must-dos: The trail is so consistently graded that you'll barely realize you are climbing and dropping more than

189

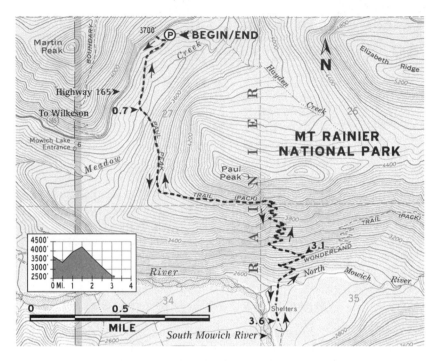

2,800 vertical feet on the walk down and back. You might also have a better chance of spotting wildlife along this trail, both in the wide flats around Meadow Creek and on the rich bottomland at the confluence of the north and south forks of the Mowich River.

The hike begins with the steepest hill first, a **0.7**-mile section down—which by no strange coincidence is up on the way home. You'll drop into the head of the flat green valley of Meadow Creek, probably the best turnaround point for families with small children. You can explore upstream from the footbridge crossing the creek to the meadows that give the creek its name. Across the creek, the trail now begins a gently graded 1.5-mile climb around the shoulder of Paul Peak. This part of the route traverses through splendid old forest on a smooth, wide trail.

As the hillside steepens, you'll approach a dry gully dropping down to the North Mowich River. The trail switches back seventeen times—down more than 1,600 vertical feet—but the grade is so consistent that you can often see two or three switchbacks ahead. Please cut them only with your eyes. At **3.1** miles, you'll strike the junction with the Wonderland Trail. Turn right here, onto the

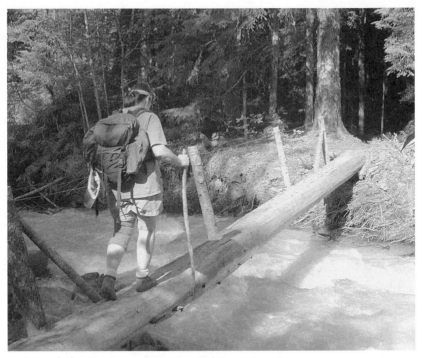

The Mowich Camp shelter makes a good
rainy-day destination on the Paul Peak Trail.

Wonderland Trail, and drop the final switchbacks down to a footlog crossing of the river.

You'll cross a second branch on a footlog, and then wander
through forested bottomland to the South Mowich River, where
you'll find a shelter, campsites, and your turnaround point, 3.6
miles from the trailhead.

50. Tolmie Peak

RATING	𝕏 𝕏 𝕏
DISTANCE	6.2 miles round-trip
HIKING TIME	3.5 hours
ELEVATION GAIN	1,120 feet
HIGH POINT	5,939 feet
DIFFICULTY LEVEL	Difficult
BEST SEASON	August; accessible July to October
PERMITS/CONTACT	Entrance fee; no day-hiking passes required; Carbon River Ranger Station, (360) 829-9639
MAPS	Green Trails No. 269, Mount Rainier West; USGS Carbon River
TRAIL NOTES	Not a good choice for kids

The Hike

This walk to beautiful alpine meadows around a clear alpine lake, followed by a tough climb to an old fire lookout, could be one of the finest hikes in the park, except for the part of the foot-worn trail in horrid condition.

Getting There

From Wilkeson, follow Highway 165 south for 9 miles to a junction with the Carbon River Road. Continue right (south) on the highway, and proceed about 12 miles to the Paul Peak trailhead on the right (south) side of the road, elevation 3,700 feet. You'll find an unmanned fee station at the parking area where you can pay the park entrance fee if you don't have an annual pass. Continue another 5.3 miles to the Mowich Lake parking area. The Tolmie Peak trailhead, elevation 4,950 feet, is located at the west end of the lake on the left, just as the road flattens above the lake. Park along the north side of the road, or continue to the larger parking area at the east end of the lake and add about 0.6 mile round-trip to the hike.

The Trail

Your feet will tell you this trail is longer than it really is, the result of a 0.5-mile climb up to Eunice Lake that is more root and mud than trail. Though this trek is often recommended as a good hike for families with small children, your kids might have more fun if you took them to a big tar pit and threw them in.

But for that section of trail, this hike would earn a much higher rating. The meadows around Eunice Lake are a kaleidoscope of wildflowers, the lake a spectacular mirror for Rainier, the Tolmie Peak lookout a fine spot from which to view the northeast side of Rainier and just about everything else in the galaxy. The hike begins with a walk along the west shoreline of Mowich Lake, with peek-a-boo views of Rainier and across the lake. The trail climbs in 0.2 mile to a low pass, switches back, and traverses through forest to the Ipsut Pass Trail junction, 1.0 mile from the trailhead.

You'll stay left at the junction, but for a good view of the Carbon River and Ipsut Creek valleys, follow the trail right a short way to Ipsut Pass. After that, the Ipsut Pass Trail drops very steeply in 0.8 mile to the Really Big Tree, Hike 45.

Back on the Tolmie Peak Trail, you'll traverse underneath cliffs on a gentle descent for about three-quarters of a mile to a wide, wet gully where the trail switchbacks up to the meadows around Eunice

Lake. Here the path widens and wettens as hikers have attempted to circumnavigate slippery mud and roots, in some places carving little more than a wide dirt or mud road up the hillside. This portion of the trail is short, however, and is easily forgotten once you reach the meadows around Eunice Lake, 2.2 miles from the trailhead.

The lake is a good spot to picnic and turn around if you've brought the youngsters. For the 600-foot climb to the lookout, stay left at the Eunice Lake Trail junction and follow the path through meadows to the west end of the lake. The trail climbs in three switchbacks to a ridge and follows the ridge to the lookout, 3.1 miles from the trailhead.

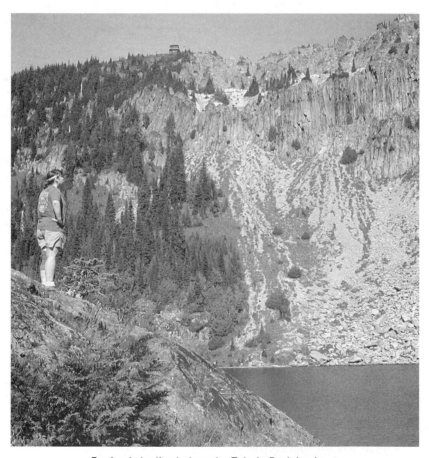

Eunice Lake lies below the Tolmie Peak Lookout.

51. Spray Park

RATING	🚶🚶🚶🚶🚶
DISTANCE	6.0 miles round-trip
HIKING TIME	3.0 to 4.0 hours
ELEVATION GAIN	2,200 feet
HIGH POINT	About 5,800 feet
DIFFICULTY LEVEL	Moderate
BEST SEASON	Late July to August; accessible mid-July through October
PERMITS/CONTACT	Entrance fee; no day-hiking passes required; Carbon River Ranger Station, (360) 829-9639
MAPS	Green Trails No. 269, Mount Rainier West; USGS Carbon River
TRAIL NOTES	No dogs or bikes; good for older kids

The Hike

One of Mount Rainier's premier—and most popular—wildflower hikes, Spray Park is a broad parkland reached by a moderately steep trail with a grand waterfall thrown in for good measure.

Lilies paint the ground of Spray Park white every spring.

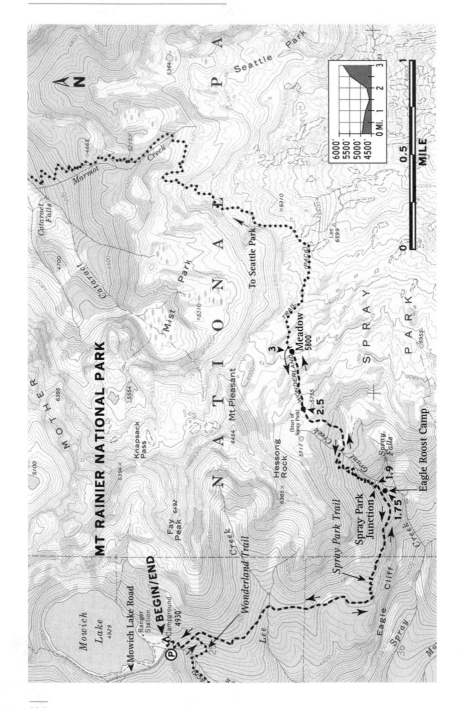

Getting There

From Wilkeson, follow Highway 165 south for 9 miles to a junction with the Carbon River Road. Continue right (south) on the highway, and proceed about 12 miles to the Paul Peak trailhead on the right (south) side of the road, elevation 3,700 feet. You'll find an unmanned fee station at the parking area where you can pay the park entrance fee if you don't have an annual pass. Continue another 5.3 miles to the Mowich Lake parking area, elevation 4,930 feet. Look for the well-signed Wonderland Trail trailhead near the lake at the south end of the parking lot.

The Trail

There is no "there" here, which is just as well, because the splendor is, well, everywhere. That's our way of saying there's no official beginning or ending to Spray Park, the destination on this stellar hike. But you'll know it when you see the signs: a sprawling corridor of open meadows with unobstructed views of Mount Rainier and the North Mowich Glacier, dozens of sparkling tarns, squadrons of whistling marmots and—assuming you arrive in July and August along with most everyone else—acre after acre of splendiferous wildflowers.

The hike begins at Mowich Lake on the Wonderland Trail, beyond the restrooms and walk-in campground. Walk **0.25** mile downhill to a junction with the Spray Park Trail. Stay left, and you're off through

Skiers descend through Spray Park after a day on the Flett Glacier.

the woods and on your way. The trail goes up and down in the first mile, south through a forest below Hessong Rock, before coming to a way trail at 1.5 miles. It leads a short distance to Eagle Cliff, a fine mountain viewpoint showcasing the North Mowich Glacier.

After you've had a look, head up the main trail about another 0.2 mile, to another spur leading a short distance south to Eagle Roost Camp, the only backcountry campsite in this area. Just beyond Eagle Roost Camp is a short spur trail to Spray Falls. You can't see the entire falls from here, but it's a big one, and definitely worth the extra steps. Besides, you'll need a quick rest before the final climb back on the main trail, which switchbacks through the forest, now on a *very* steep grade toward Spray Park. Pace yourself: The trail is about 600 feet on nearly two dozen switchbacks over the final 0.5 mile to the meadows.

It's worth it, though. Soon, the trees will begin to fall away and the blue-sky spaces get larger. Before you know it, you're in the clear, entering Spray Park—a vast, rolling plain of tarns, rocky outcrops, and alpine greenery about 2.5 miles from the trailhead. If you hit it right, there may be no better wildflower treasure trove in the entire park, and perhaps on the entire planet. You can stop at the first meadows, but it's worth walking the extra 0.5 mile or so to the sprawling meadowland beneath 6,454-foot Mount Pleasant, to the north.

The parkland all around here begs to be explored by foot, but please keep in mind the damage your oversized lug soles do to fragile alpine meadows. Stay on established trails, find a good lunch spot, and soak up the splendor. Go as far as you like, but keep in mind that snow often lingers on the upper route well into August. The way is marked by cairns and wands, but don't venture too far if you're uncomfortable with, or ill-equipped for, snow travel.

Going Farther

If you proceed higher into the meadows, the trail tops out at a ridge at 6,400 feet, about 4 miles from the trailhead. Here, it begins its descent toward Seattle Park and the Carbon River drainage. Some strong hikers with a shuttle car used to like to hike beyond the high point another 2.6 miles north, through Seattle Park and past Cataract Camp to end at Ipsut Creek Campground (see Hike 47) for a total through hike of about 11.5 miles. But you'll now have to add another 5 miles of hike/bike travel to get to that shuttle car, thanks to the closure of the Carbon River Road to auto traffic.

INDEX